PREPARING

DIGITAL IMAGES

FOR PRINT

SYBIL IHRIG • EMIL IHRIG

Osborne **McGraw-Hill**

Berkeley   New York   St. Louis   San Francisco
Auckland   Bogotá   Hamburg   London   Madrid
Mexico City   Milan   Montreal   New Delhi   Panama City
Paris   São Paulo   Singapore   Sydney
Tokyo   Toronto

Osborne **McGraw-Hill**
2600 Tenth Street
Berkeley, California 94710
U.S.A.

For information on translations or book distributors outside the U.S.A., or to arrange bulk purchase discounts for sales promotions, premiums, or fundraisers, please contact Osborne **McGraw-Hill** at the above address.

Preparing Digital Images for Print

1234567890 DOC 99876

ISBN 0-07-882146-0

Executive Editor:	Scott Rogers
Project Editor:	Emily Rader
Copy Editor:	Ann Kameoka
Proofreader:	Linda Medoff
Cover Design:	Ted Mader & Associates
Cover Photo (center):	Emil Ihrig, VersaTech Associates
Series Design:	Emil Ihrig, VersaTech Associates
Page Composition:	Sybil Ihrig, VersaTech Associates

About the Authors...

Sybil and Emil Ihrig of VersaTech Associates are prepress and production experts; Emil Ihrig is also a professional photographer and digital photoillustrator. The Ihrigs are authors of books on several subjects, including scanning, CorelDRAW!, QuarkXpress, and PhotoStyler. Their company, VersaTech Associates, designs and produces books for major publishers throughout the United States. They can be reached on America Online (sybilihrig), on CompuServe (72730,1153), and on the Internet (sybilihrig@aol.com.).

Dedication:

For Angela, Jason, and Corey—with love

Contents

Screening and Print Reproduction Basics *25*

Color Reproduction and Management *39*

Image-Editing and Enhancement Tools *63*

Color Separations and Conversions *75*

Tonal Correction for Output   97

Balancing and Correcting Color   113

Resolution and Sizing for Print Media   129

Sharpening and Special-Case Adjustments   *141*

Foreword

Someone once said that an amateur photographer or artist might make a thousand failed attempts on the way to creating a single masterpiece. A professional, on the other hand, does not have a mandate to create a masterpiece, but every attempt must, at the very least, measure up to a marketable standard. Professionals can't afford to rely on happy accidents to satisfy a demanding client.

But let's face it: Even for the most proficient of designers, the burden of the creative process alone can be overwhelming at times. Today's added responsibilities include, at the very least, image color and tone manipulations and specifying color separation parameters. Even the most experienced graphic artists can get the jitters when they alone are accountable for the printed results of their number crunching.

In the not-so-distant old days, the separation house might have afforded designers a certain comfort level by taking on the responsibility for producing high-quality film and plates. These days, however, lacking the reassurance that the stereotypical, cigar-chomping tradeshop pro somehow managed to offer a beleaguered designer, designers must now fend for themselves—plugging numbers into arcane dialog boxes and hoping that they will not be victimized by phenomena as mystical as metameric shift or as mundane as dot gain.

Of course, there is always the other side of the coin—the beleaguered service bureau or color house professional who is now victimized by designers infused with their newfound power, yet somehow not quite knowledgeable enough to use it wisely. Such customers are the bane of the tradeshop, with their overly-grouped vector files that take hours to trap and rip, and their overly-sharpened, under-resolution scans. How do you keep customers when you have to tell them that the poor-quality results are their fault, not yours?

Living on both sides of this fence, Sybil and Emil Ihrig have committed themselves to negotiating an understanding, a neutral zone where the common ground of communication arms the designer and separator alike with the knowledge, the terminology, and the tools they need to produce fine work consistently—both as individuals and as a team.

The practice of print reproduction represents a marriage of art and science, a combination of skill and aesthetic understanding. As such, it is both mechanical and creative at the same time.

Some of us have experienced the euphoria associated with developing an image in the darkroom. From the stark white emptiness of light-sensitive paper comes an image, emerging under the red glow in thin, veiled tones, until gradually the deeper shadows take on their fullness with breathtaking impact. For many of us in the graphic arts, that remarkable sensation never really goes away, no matter how many times we repeat the process. Even today, unjaded by years of commercial practice, the experience of photographic printmaking is still ethereal for me, except that now I can get my kicks from the more overwhelming process of reproducing pictures on press.

Until recently, photographic printmaking was the only type of printmaking that was accessible to the average photographer. Only those who could afford large-scale four-color reproduction were privileged to share in the mystique of lithography or gravure.

That certainly has changed. We in the trenches are now able to get the same jollies we used to get in the darkroom—only this time we can do it on press, because technology has given us inexpensive tools that permit the luxury of creating, preparing, and reproducing personal work (or the work of others) on our desktops.

Graphic artists and professional photographers alike have traditionally left the mysteries of the printing press to the wizards. That has often led to disputes over who is to blame for poor results. Finger pointing is usually the prerogative of those who pay for the job, but costly mistakes don't foster a satisfying outcome, since cost has a lot to do with warm and fuzzy feelings (or the absence thereof).

These days, I might miss the pleasure I used to get from photographic processing, except that I have replaced that stimulus with a new sensual gratification. For me, the darkroom now has its parallel in the pressroom, with all the sensory overload one derives from the olfactory assault of powerful printing ink solvents, the smell and feel of expensive paper stocks, the reverberating roar of a six-color web press, and the sheer power of dazzling saturated colors that seem more real than reality itself.

In this handsomely designed and lavishly illustrated book, prepress experts Sybil and Emil Ihrig explain the mystique of the print reproduction process as it applies to digital images. They have debunked misleading mythology and disclosed many truly practicable techniques to make the printing experience creative, enjoyable, and above all, thoroughly predictable in terms of the quality of the results you can achieve. After completing this book, not only will you feel that you really understand how images are reproduced in print and how you can best control the process; you will want to refer to it again and again.

Preparing Digital Images for Print represents a milestone in desktop prepress education. Sybil and Emil Ihrig have taken an unusually invigorating approach to clarifying the realm of desktop color. Their explanations are refreshingly concide, presented in an eminently readable format that lends itself to understanding the visual effects of each manipulation. This is by no means a simple recipe book to be blindly obeyed; it is a comprehensive guide to print reproduction that will help anyone in the fields of graphic design, production, illustration, or photography develop an ability to previsualize their work, from the initial concept to rewarding, professional-looking results. Sybil and Emil have done it again. Congratulations on a most rewarding work!

John Harcourt
Strategic Marketing Manager
Nikon Electronic Imaging
April, 1996

Acknowledgments

We love to make graphic designers, photographers, artists, other authors, and their respective publishers look good in print; that's why we got into the business of production in the first place. In writing this book, our aim has been to help others who are entrusted with the challenges of print output make *their* respective clients look good, too. Many individuals, corporations, and associations have assisted us in this quest, and we'd like to thank as many of them as our memories can accommodate.

Thanks go first to Osborne/McGraw-Hill's Executive Editor, Scott Rogers, who acquired this title and very, very patiently waited for its completion (albeit with the requisite weekly cattle prod) during its incubation period while we had to put out production fires. Our Editorial Assistant, Daniela Dell'Orco, accomplished level-headed scheduling tasks with great tact and warmth and jumped in just before press time to play the additional role of advertising coordinator. We also appreciated Project Editor Emily Rader's regular communications; she deserves special commendation for so efficiently coordinating copyediting and proofreading tasks in the avalanche of manuscript and proofs that snowed her during the last three weeks before shipping the book to press. Thanks also to Anne Ellingsen and Polly Fusco for unearthing some interesting publicity and sales opportunities, to Claudia Ramirez for so adeptly arousing the interest of the international market in our book, and to always-upbeat Deborah Wilson for her ongoing trust and steady support of our design and production efforts.

We appreciate all the suggestions that our technical editor, John Harcourt of Nikon Electronic Imaging, presented from the perspective of a commercial photographer and digital photography adept. Thanks for the many online insights and discussions. Thanks, too, to Herb Paynter of ImageXPress for making the initial introduction to John and for supplying several of the technical graphics used in Chapters 3 and 9.

In such a fast-changing technical field, it would have been impossible to achieve the level of depth at which we aimed without the support and communications we received from equipment and software manufacturers and industry associations. Thanks especially to Deborah Bolton at ViewSonic Corporation for allowing us to work with the excellent PT810, Barbara Trost at Light Source, the Graphic Arts Technical Foundation, Don Orr and the prelim staff at R.R. Donnelley & Sons,

Stephen Herron at Isis Imaging, and Richard Kraus at Tektronix. We also want to thank 3M, Adobe, Agfa, Apple Computer, DayStar Digital, Dicomed, Eastman Kodak, Fargo, Human Software, MetaTools, Micronet, Nikon Electronic Imaging, PhotoDisc, Polaroid Corporation, SyQuest International, UMAX, Wacom, Westlight, and Yamaha for providing information and literature. If we've inadvertently omitted anyone, please excuse our oversight.

Finally, we want to thank our families for their patience and understanding during the many months when they had to put up with the litany of "Sorry, I don't have time to talk now," and "No, we haven't written—we're writing!"

We hope that the following pages will amply repay all of you for the efforts and communications so generously given to assist us in this project. And we invite readers to contact us via e-mail with comments and questions.

Sybil and Emil Ihrig, VersaTech Associates
sybilihrig@aol.com
72730,1153 (CompuServe)

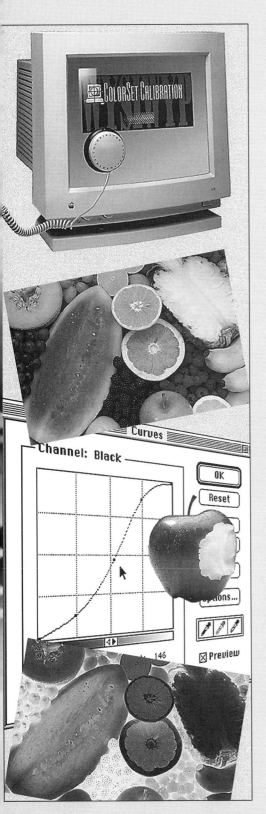

Consider
the Source

Ensuring impeccable print quality for our digital images is the holy grail of graphic design. Producing images for print may be more of an art than a science, but that doesn't stop us from wishing for a foolproof roadmap to the desired destination. Fortunately, there *are* reliable signposts you can count on to help you reach your goal. This book documents each of those signposts to aid you in obtaining the highest-quality results for your images on press.

One key guidepost involves the characteristics of the *source image*—the artwork you start out with, which may or may not already be in digital form. What goes up must come down, and what comes out of a printer, imagesetter, platesetter, or printing press must have originated from a computer. How it got there reveals much, both about the limits of quality you can expect from the image and about the steps you should take to prepare it for printing. In this chapter, we'll consider the most common sources of digital images—scanners, digital cameras, Photo CD, digital stock photos, and video and screen captures—and examine what you should keep in mind when preparing each type for print output.

❝You should know as much as possible at the time of scanning about your project's eventual output and press parameters.❞

Scanned Images

Many factors influence the quality of a scanned image. Among them are the type of original scanned, the technical capabilities of the scanner, the skill of the scanner operator, the size of the original relative to the enlargement needed, the scanning resolution, and any processing applied to the image during scanning. Whether you're doing the scanning yourself or hiring the services of a service bureau or color house, you owe it to the success of your print projects to educate yourself in minute detail about how your scans are obtained. Above all, if you want scanned images to turn out well, you should know as much as possible at the time of scanning about your project's eventual output and press parameters such as output size, halftone screen frequency, paper stock, press type, tonal limits, and expected dot gain. Matching those parameters to the foregoing factors will truly ensure that every scan is a quality scan. For more in-depth information on scanning for the highest-quality results, see *Scanning the Professional Way* (Berkeley, CA: Osborne/McGraw-Hill, 1995).

Medium of Original

The medium of an original can help you determine the kind of scanner that should be used to digitize it and the processing steps required to prepare the scan for print.

Density

When determining how an original should be scanned, its *density*—the ability of a material to absorb, reflect, or transmit light, measured as a value between 0 and 4.0—is an important attribute to consider. Originals fall into two broad categories, *reflective* media and *transmissive* media. Reflective media, which include previously printed artwork, hand-drawn illustrations on paper, and photographic prints, have densities ranging from approximately 1.0 to 2.3. Flatbed scanners can easily capture all the tonal gradations in such low-density originals. Transmissive media include negative films (density 2.8), color slides (density 2.7 to 3.0), and larger-format transparencies (density 3.0 to 3.2). If transmissive originals are your main stock in trade, film/transparency scanners and drum scanners are the best choices for digitizing them. Match the density attributes of your most frequently digitized originals to the dynamic range of a particular scanner for the highest-quality results (see the "Color Depth and Dynamic Range" section of this chapter).

Note: *Very few films exceed densities of 3.2. One exception is Vericolor print film (density approaching 4.0), which is designed for making motion picture prints and transparencies from negatives.*

Special Processing Needs

The medium of an original also affects the kind of processing its digital counterpart will require, either during scanning or in an image-editing package later. Solid-color logos and illustrations, for example, are best scanned in line art or gray-scale mode; previously printed artwork requires the use of a descreening filter to remove existing halftone patterning; and all scanned images need sharpening. Negative film has a strong apparent *color cast* (a pervasive, undesired tint), which must be compensated for either by the scanner or later through color correction.

Note: *The "cast" apparent in color negative film is actually a mask layer, the purpose of which is to rebalance tungsten-lighted exposures.*

Scanner Type and Characteristics

The capabilities of the scanner you use to digitize an original constrains the limits of quality you can obtain in print. You wouldn't want to enter the Indy 500 driving a golf cart; neither would you need a Ferrari to deliver pizza locally. By the same token, a low-end or midrange flatbed scanner couldn't deliver the tonal range necessary for high-end advertising, but obtaining drum scans for newsprint catalogs wouldn't be a smart use of your scanning dollar, either. Capabilities among manufacturers vary, even within the same scanner class, but the essential characteristics to evaluate are the quality of a scanner's sensing device, its maximum optical resolution, the types of media it can accept, its maximum color depth, and its dynamic range.

Sensing Technology

All scanners use one of two types of sensing technologies. *Charge-coupled devices* (*CCDs*) are found in flatbed and film/transparency scanners, while *photomultiplier tubes* (*PMTs*) are the mainstay of drum scanners. (See our companion title, *Scanning the Professional Way*, for an in-depth treatment of what makes each technology tick.) PMT technology makes it possible for an extremely bright light source to focus on one tiny area of an image at a time, which in turn lets drum scanners reproduce all the tones in even the densest originals.

With electronic CCD sensors, the light sensitivity of the individual sensors and their relative insulation from electrical and other ambient noise are the major limiting factors. The artifacts and noise often observed on CCD-scanned images stem from electrical circuit instability and a phenomenon called *dark current*—a constant flow of electrical signals to the sensors, which makes it difficult to obtain clean detail in the darkest areas of a positive image. Sensor quality generally varies according to cost. For the cleanest, most artifact-free scans, look for a flatbed or transparency scanner that has a high *signal-to-noise ratio*, a specification that indicates the strength of sensor signals relative to ambient noise. CCD sensors are arranged in linear *arrays* (single horizontal rows of sensors) for flatbed scanners and in linear or rectangular arrays for film/transparency scanners.

Optical Resolution and Imaging Area

In print publishing, the amount of data in a digital image counts for as much as the physical dimensions at which it will be output (see Chapter 9). Together, the optical resolution and imaging area of a scanner determine how much data can be captured for an original of a given size. *Optical resolution*, usually measured in pixels or dots per inch (ppi or dpi), defines the maximum amount of data that a given scanner can sample per linear inch or centimeter. *Imaging area* defines the size of the largest original that a scanner can accept. Knowing the optical resolution of a scanner, its imaging area, and the degree of enlargement required for a given original will tell you whether the scanner you have in mind has the horsepower to perform the job well. Reflective originals come in all sizes and can be digitized by flatbed and drum scanners; transmissive originals have fixed sizes and are best scanned by a film/transparency scanner or drum scanner, both of which are capable of the high resolutions needed to enlarge small transmissives many times.

Ideally, you should scan an image with exactly the right amount of data for good print output. This can happen only if the scanner operator knows three things in advance: the final print dimensions of the image, the halftone screen frequency required for output, and the resolution (in dpi) of the imagesetter or platesetter that will generate the final output. See *Scanning the Professional Way* for tips on how to calculate the proper scanning resolution for any print project.

Caution: Avoid scanning at interpolated resolutions—*resolutions higher than the maximum optical resolution of which a scanner is capable. Interpolation adds extra pixels through a mathematical averaging process but doesn't add new detail. Get a more powerful scanner if your scanner's optical resolution doesn't support the amount of enlargement you require.*

Note: Although some midrange flatbeds can *scan transmissives, their light sources can't provide even, edge-to-edge illumination across the width of the imaging area. The color quality of the illumination source and signal-to-noise ratio are other important limiting factors. Only high-end flatbeds such as those found at some color prepress houses have the optical resolution, the optimum light source characteristics, and the noise compensation technology required to scan slides and transparencies well.*

Color Depth and Dynamic Range

Bit depth and *color depth* express (in powers of two) the maximum number of color or gray levels a scanning device can sense for each pixel that it samples. When you scan in 1-bit (2^1) mode, all the pixels in the resulting image are either black or white. Scanning in grayscale (8-bit) mode produces up to 256 shades of gray, and scanning in RGB (24-bit) mode reproduces up to 16,777,216 (2^{24}) colors. So-called CMYK scans—handled automatically by most drum scanners, and through software by some flatbed and film/transparency scanners—are actually RGB scans that are then immediately color separated.

Drum scanners, and a growing number of flatbed and film/transparency scanners, are capable of *high-bit* scanning. This means that the scanner's image-sensing circuit discerns a far higher number of potential tonal levels per pixel than 16 million; the scanner's processors may then sample this number down to a "normal" 24-bit range, or to a higher bit range. The result, theoretically at least, is a broader *dynamic range* (brightness range) for the images digitized by the scanner, and thus better differentiation between adjacent tones in shadows (for positive originals; see Figure 1–1) or highlights (for negative originals). In practice, though, an image with a nominally broad dynamic range from a scanner that doesn't have a high signal-to-noise ratio can still be full of unsightly artifacts.

Types of Scanners

There are three basic types of scanners in commercial use: drum scanners, flatbed scanners, and film/transparency scanners. Each type is best suited to specific output needs, but beware—the quality distinctions between these three types are less clear cut than they used to be, especially at higher price ranges.

Drum scanners have long been regarded as the scanners of choice for high-end color print jobs such as advertising materials, annual reports, and fine art reproductions. Their acute PMT sensing technology lets them capture even the subtlest tones in any type of original; they can digitize both reflective and transparent originals (excepting negative films) at high color depths; and they are capable of extremely high resolutions, which permit small originals to be enlarged many times without degradation. Most drum scanners also feature sophisticated software controls that automatically process images for press conditions on the fly during scanning. Once the province of color prepress houses only, drum scanners are now available in desktop-sized configurations that connect seamlessly to a Macintosh or Windows-based PC (see Figure 1–2). If you regularly print documents with demanding color requirements and need to scan a high volume of positive originals, it may pay to obtain your digital images from drum scanners.

Flatbed scanners use CCD sensing technology, which varies greatly in the quality of its implementation. The CCDs in low-cost and midrange flatbed scanners tend to be susceptible to noise, which can result in visible artifacts such as scan lines or stray pixels of the "wrong" color. Higher-end flatbeds used in some service bureaus and corporations use CCD sensors that are better insulated from noise

Figure 1–1

© Emil Ihrig

A positive original scanned by equipment that has a high dynamic range (top) shows good detail even in the shadow tones. The same original digitized by a scanner that has a lower dynamic range (bottom) shows higher contrast and a lack of detail in comparable tonal areas.

and therefore produce cleaner scans. Flatbeds are especially well suited to digitizing *reflective* artwork such as photographic prints and line drawings. Midrange and higher-end flatbeds can also scan transmissive originals, but only the highest-end flatbeds can reproduce them with the same quality as a drum or film/transparency scanner. These days, scans from midrange and higher-end flatbeds offer acceptable quality for use in

Figure 1–2

courtesy Screen USA

The Screen 1015AI entry-level desktop drum scanner offers intelligent image analysis and enhancement. Features include input resolutions up to 2,500 ppi, on-the-fly CMYK scanning and sharpening, 30-bit color depth, and an imaging area of 5.8 × 5.9 inches.

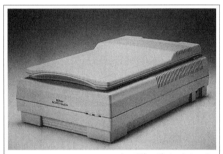

courtesy Nikon Electronic Imaging

courtesy UMAX

Figure 1–3

The Nikon ScanTouch (top), a 600 × 1,200 ppi scanner, processes 10 bits per color down to a clean 8 bits per color. The UMAX PowerLook (bottom) claims a dynamic range of 3.0 and a maximum optical resolution of 600 × 1,200 ppi. Both models offer an optional transparency unit for digitizing transmissive originals.

most commercial-grade color documents and periodicals. Figure 1–3 shows two midrange flatbed scanners.

- *Film and transparency scanners,* though they are CCD-based like flatbeds, use more sensitive sensors and are capable of much higher resolutions—characteristics that make them ideal for digitizing small transmissive originals. Many such scanners feature a dynamic range high enough to capture the full range of tones available in the average transmissive. In fact, for most commercial-grade color print jobs, you'd be hard pressed to discern much of a difference between a drum-scanned image and one scanned using a film/transparency scanner with high-quality sensors (for an example, see the Color Gallery of *Scanning the Professional Way*). Midrange and higher-end film/transparency scanners automatically correct for the apparent color casts of negative film. Figure 1–4 shows examples of midrange film/transparency scanners that digitize both negative film and slides.

Preprocessing

An increasing number of scanners of all types have built-in *preprocessing* capabilities for adjusting image tone, color, and sharpness during the scanning process itself. If a scanner's preprocessing options are sophisticated enough, an image can be ready for printing as soon as

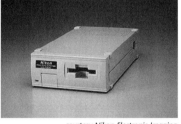

courtesy Polaroid Corporation   *courtesy Nikon Electronic Imaging*

Figure 1–4

With a claimed dynamic range of 3.0, the Polaroid SprintScan35 (left) digitizes positive and negative 35 mm originals at resolutions of up to 2,700 ppi in less than a minute. The equally speedy Nikon Super-CoolScan (right) senses color at 36 bits. Both units can reproduce the entire dynamic range of transparent media cleanly.

it's scanned. Preprocessing can save you valuable production time, but only if you know all the print parameters for a project at the time of scanning *and* the scanner's image-processing features are as advanced as those of your favorite image-editing package. Unless both of these conditions hold true for you, you're better off applying *no* on-the-fly processing to the image and handling image-correction tasks as a postprocessing step in your usual software.

Photo CD Images

Initially conceived as a consumer product, Photo CD has found its natural home in the graphic arts community. Photo CD is rapidly becoming the favored method of image acquisition among many catalog, magazine, and book publishers. When compared with drum scans, Photo CD offers high-volume storage for low cost in a medium that's easy to transfer from one party to another. Now that Kodak has made its Image Pac format an open standard, Photo CD stands to become even more popular as a means of image acquisition for print media professionals.

Although the basic process of producing Photo CDs is standardized, the quality of service varies from one provider to another. If you want Photo CD images to match the color characteristics of the original film or transparencies closely, ask the provider to process the scans using a *universal film term* setting that doesn't correct for film type, and entrust the job to a custom photo finishing lab rather than to a mass-market provider. If, on the other hand, you want the resulting images to have standardized memory colors (see Chapter 8) regardless of what type of film was used in the originals, request that the Photo CD provider observe the principle of scene balance.

Enhancing Photo CD Images on the Fly

The workflow for preparing Photo CD images for print differs from the workflow for scanned images; the best time to correct a Photo CD image is on the fly when you acquire it, not later in the production process. This difference in workflow is due partly to Photo CD's origins in the photographic world—images are generated with film, not printing presses, in mind—and partly to the fact that images are usually opened into the RGB or CMYK color space, even though they were encoded onto disc using the YCC color space (see Chapter 4). There are many ways to open a Photo CD image into an image-editing program, and the method you choose impacts the range of colors you extract. This can be critical for print output quality, since any color correction made *after* acquiring and saving the image results in loss of data and excessive tonal compression.

Opinions differ about the best way to acquire a Photo CD image. Kodak's CMS plug-in, provided with Adobe Photoshop and Micrografx Picture Publisher, offers a robust YCC-to-RGB color conversion but permits no color correction prior to acquisition. The Kodak Acquire and Access Plus modules do offer on-the-fly color correction options, but their color space conversion algorithms are reportedly less sophisticated, unless you boost them up with add-on utilities such as DMMS's PhotoStep and Kodak's Precision Transforms starter kit.

More promising are third-party plug-ins and full-fledged software packages that perform sharpening, color correction, and YCC-to-CMYK conversion on the fly in accordance with the print output parameters you specify. CD/Q and CD/Q Batch from the Human Software Company and Display Technologies' PhotoImpress (Figure 1–5) handle these tasks; PhotoImpress also includes color management software that optimizes the conversion between

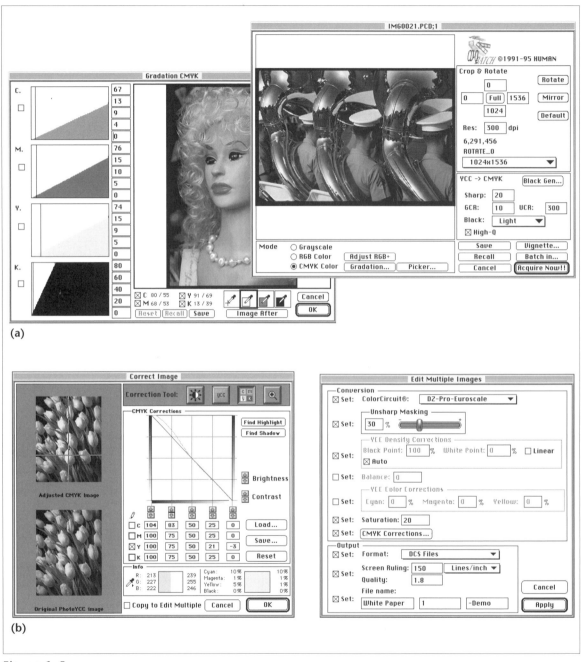

Figure 1–5

*Human Software's CD/Q Batch (**a**) performs sharpening, color correction, and CMYK conversion of multiple Photo CD images during the acquisition process. PhotoImpress from Display Technologies (**b**) handles similar tasks with lightning speed and also includes built-in color management.*

color spaces. This strategy works only if you're familiar with the output specifications for your project in advance.

If you use Adobe Photoshop and don't have the funds to invest in a third-party package like those just described, you can minimize quality loss by opening Photo CD images in Photoshop's LAB color mode and performing some of the necessary corrections there. LAB color isn't the most intuitive mode to work in, but it *is* effective for sharpening, as you'll see in Chapter 10.

Images from Digital Cameras

Once considered heretical by professional photographers, digital cameras are rapidly gaining a niche in print publishing, particularly among catalog and newspaper publishers. They offer the advantages of lower cost per shoot (no film, fewer color separation cycles) and reduced production time (no waiting for film development and scanning). There's another significant advantage for catalog publishers; digital cameras offer better swatch-matching color accuracy than a film-and-scanning workflow can achieve.

There are two distinct types of digital cameras—*scan-back* and *array* cameras, each suited for different uses (see Figure 1–6). Both types use CCD sensors to record an image. But that's where the similarity ends. The sensors in scan-back, or scanning, cameras are configured in a single *linear array* that scans the subject slowly like a flatbed scanner, one narrow horizontal strip at a time. Linear arrays permit these cameras to deliver hefty amounts of data suitable for large print dimensions; but image capture is correspondingly slow, and these cameras must be tethered to a computer during the shoot. Their lack of portability, slow capture times, and lack of sensitivity to available light make scan-back cameras suitable for still photography only. Like analog time-exposure cameras, they're also sensitive to vibration; make sure your digital studio contains no sources of vibration if you want to maximize the sharpness of your image captures.

The sensors in array cameras, on the other hand, are arranged in a rectangular *tri-color array*. The fixed number of sensors in array cameras makes near-instantaneous

courtesy Dicomed

courtesy Nikon Electronic Imaging

Figure 1–6

*The Dicomed Digital Camera Back (**top**) is a 4 x 5 scanning camera that can capture images with resolutions of up to 6,000 x 7,520 pixels in 2 to 13 minutes. The Nikon ES2/Fujix DS-515 array camera (**bottom**), with an ISO sensitivity of 1,600 for low-light photography, can expose seven consecutive frames at three frames per second in continuous mode and uses removable PCMCIA cards as image storage devices.*

capture possible, even as it limits image resolution (and thus maximum print output size). The advent of PCMCIA cards and other portable storage devices has liberated these cameras from the computer's umbilical cord; the best of them can be used for both action and still photography.

CCD sensors are subject to noise; and in array cameras, the longer the exposure times, the more likely noise artifacts are to appear. For the best output results, use despeckling or noise-minimizing filters on the captures, particularly in the blue channel where noise is more prevalent.

Digital Stock Photos

Until recently, the concept of *stock photography* meant obtaining professionally photographed slides or transparencies from an agency for fees negotiated on a per-use basis. Today's options are much more varied. You can search for the perfect image online; buy royalty-free CD-ROM collections of photographs, backgrounds, or textures outright; or obtain a sampler CD of a stock-agency's collection in low-resolution format, then negotiate for the high-resolution versions of images you choose. When saved as TIFFs, digital stock photos require the same types of prepress enhancement as scanned images; when saved in the Kodak Image Pac format, they should be enhanced like Photo CD images.

Royalty-Free Collections

Open the display advertising section at the back of any magazine related to desktop publishing, design, or photography, and you'll see a steadily growing number of companies offering royalty-free collections of stock images on CD-ROM (Figure 1–7). Typically, each CD in a collection focuses on a specific theme. Vendors also offer unique types of images that are suited to the way today's

Figure 1–7

*Sample royalty-free stock images from HSC Software's KPT Power Photos collection (**left**) and Clement Mok Productions' CMCD Stock (**right**). Both collections feature single-subject images that are suitable for electronic compositing. The subjects contain previously constructed masks or clipping paths to facilitate filtering, processing, and printing.*

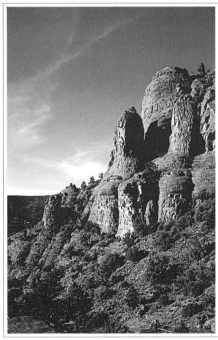

courtesy MetaTools, Inc.

designers composite images electronically—textures or backgrounds, for example, or single-subject images that are already masked (*premasked*) to make filtering and compositing easier. Usually, images are stored in either Photo CD or RGB TIFF format and are accompanied by a run-time version of image database software that allows you to search and preview images. Image quality may vary; most vendors have little background in traditional stock photography.

With royalty-free collections, the purchaser pays a one-time fee for the disc itself and then may use images therein to visually enhance another product, as long as that product isn't offered for sale or profit. Most collections restrict usage to a certain extent; for example, you may be prohibited from using images in a pornographic or defamatory context. You may have to pay per-use royalties if you publish the image in a calendar or other context in which the image itself is the main subject of resale.

Stock Agency Collections

A growing number of traditional stock photo agencies now provide either high-resolution images or low-resolution catalogs of their analog photos on CD-ROM. Digital catalogs often include navigational software to help you find an image with the desired attributes (Figure 1–8). Unlike vendors of royalty-free collections, stock agencies require that you negotiate usage fees. That may seem like a disadvantage, but keep in mind that stock agencies have hundreds of

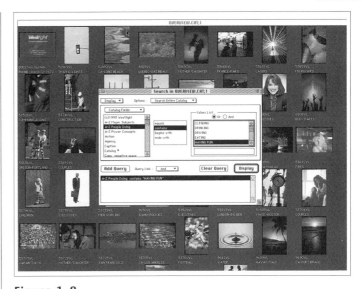

Figure 1–8

Westlight Stock Photography supplies a catalog of its stock photos on CD-ROM, complete with interactive navigational software. Photos are available as either high-resolution digital images or reproduction-quality transparencies.

thousands or even millions of images at their disposal, so you're not likely to see the same image used the same way in multiple publications. Stock agencies also have a vested interest in controlling the quality of the images they offer. For a small fee, you can obtain a listing of major stock agencies (many of whom now offer digital catalogs or images) by calling the Picture Agency Council of America (PACA) at (800) 457-7222.

Online Picture Services

A third way to obtain stock photos is through online picture services accessed by modem. Some individual stock agencies have proprietary online resources, but the trend is toward third-party services that offer images from multiple agencies. Some of these clearinghouses have Web sites on the Internet or presences on commercial online services such as CompuServe and America Online. Each service has its own navigational software for viewing thumbnails and searching for picture attributes based on keywords. In addition to usage fees for pictures selected, users typically incur charges for initial sign-up, monthly subscription, online time, and downloading of low-resolution comp images. Among the most well-known online picture services are Kodak Picture Exchange, Picture Network International's Seymour, and Knight-Ridder's PressLink, which is geared toward newspaper publishers.

Video and Computer Screen Captures

Images captured from analog video sources or computer screens contain a fixed amount of data, which limits the physical dimensions at which you can print them successfully (see Chapter 9). NTSC video (the North American standard) produces an analog signal that's equivalent to 525 × 486 pixels of information. The amount of data you can capture from a computer screen depends on the resolution of the monitor (1,024 × 768 pixels, for example).

Each source medium also presents its own set of challenges. The color scheme of video images is very different from that of RGB or CMYK color, so extensive color correction is usually necessary for print reproduction. When capturing computer screens for print output, you should use a display adapter that reproduces only pure colors without dithering. You should also use screen capture software that doesn't dither colors or shades of gray. Otherwise, the final printed images could contain unsightly *moirés* (visual interference pat-

terns) that make the publication look like an amateur job. If you can't be choosy about the source of the captures and dithering is present, you may need to replace some areas of the captures with solid colors or gray shades.

Note: *Screen capture software that uses error-diffusion dither won't produce moirés, since this type of dither is random rather than patterned.*

Original Digital Illustrations

If your print projects are to contain original raster illustrations and montage illustrations created entirely in paint or image-editing software (Figure C–1 in the Color Gallery), it's your responsibility to tell the illustrator the correct print dimensions and output resolution *before* the creative work begins. Few things are more frustrating than receiving an illustration that doesn't have enough data to print well! If the print dimensions for the piece are unknown when the creative work is taking place, specify the largest dimensions that the project could possibly use; removing information from an image is always safer than adding it.

In this chapter, we've summarized the main sources of digital images and the typical challenges they present to print production. Forge ahead to Chapter 2, where we'll provide hints on equipping your digital studio for the highest-quality results your print projects require.

2

Working the System

When producing digital images for print, the question invariably arises: How much system is enough? If your system is underpowered in terms of hardware or software, productivity and revenue can decline even as personnel and production costs go up. On the other hand, having more horsepower than your print jobs require doesn't do much for your bottom line, especially if the individuals operating the systems don't have the training or experience to make the most of your system's potential.

How Much System Is Enough?

Determining what equipment and software you need to meet image production requirements is a matter of coordinating five factors:

- The type of documents you produce
- The type of press and paper setup your documents require
- Screening technology and typical number of color separations
- The volume of work you produce on a regular basis
- Typical print dimensions for the images you produce

Let's look briefly at how each of these factors impact your ideal system setup.

Document Type and Audience Expectation

The issue of document type boils down to what kind of audience you're targeting, its budget, the type of publication that holds appeal for it, and the message you want to send. If you create high-end advertising for glossy magazines for example, then you need to court your intended audience using only the most sophisticated drum scanners, the fastest computer systems with plenty of RAM, high-volume storage solutions for those multi-megabyte files, and the latest in color proofing technologies. If you're involved in daily, weekly, or monthly production activities for newspapers, magazines, or catalogs, you might need to rely on hand-held digital cameras, somewhat less RAM (since file sizes are smaller), high-speed modem connections, and heavy-duty backup storage for long-term file archival. But if your stock-in-trade is an occasional flyer or mailer for local small businesses, you don't need such sophisticated input, output, and system capabilities.

Press Setup

The type of documents you produce, along with your publication budget, determine the combination of press and paper needed to print the job. Most types of documents that contain digital images are run on offset presses; the major exceptions are packaging and periodicals with extremely high-volume print runs, which are run on flexographic and rotogravure presses, respectively. From high end to low end, the seven distinct offset press-and-paper setups are

- Sheet-fed/coated
- Sheet-fed/uncoated
- Web offset/coated
- Web offset/uncoated
- Newspaper/coated
- Newspaper/uncoated
- Newspaper/newsprint

The more elite the setup, the more demanding (and expensive) the system, input, and output requirements are likely to be. For instance, a high-fashion catalog to be printed on coated paper on a heat-set web press would demand higher-quality image input, processing, storage, and proofing than a black-and-white catalog of merchant services printed on newsprint on a newspaper press.

> **"The more elite the press setup, the more demanding the system, input, and output requirements are likely to be."**

Screening and Separation Technology

The technology you use to reproduce the color in your digital images impacts the amount of data each image must contain and, consequently, the horsepower you need for processing. *Color separations*—the use of a few (typically four) colors on press to simulate many, many more—are a fact of life because the printing process can't reproduce the millions of colors in a digital image directly (more about that in Chapter 3). However, not all color separations are created in the same way. If you use the standard CMYK separation scheme that produces four color plates per image, file sizes may not need to be as large as you've been led to believe (see Chapter 10). However, a technology called *HiFi color*, which uses six or seven color plates to improve color saturation, is growing in popularity at the high end of the prepress market, and HiFi color separations generate substantially larger image files.

Another factor in color separation that affects image file size is the *screening* technology used to simulate so many colors. Digital halftone screening runs the risk of color *registration* (alignment) problems on press, so various forms of *stochastic* screening have been developed to place halftone dots on a page in a way that will make the issue of registration less critical. Some professionals feel that stochastic screening permits the use of lower output resolutions and smaller file sizes than conventional halftone screening (see Chapter 3).

Note: *Regardless of the screening method, misregistration always produces "soft," unsharp print.*

Volume of Work

If you must prepare a large number of images for print on a daily, weekly, or even monthly basis, having input and output devices in-house—scanners, color printers, color proofing systems, imagesetters—becomes more cost-effective than to send out for prepress services. But if you handle a small volume of work on a less regular basis, you may not be able to justify the cost of the extra equipment.

Print Dimensions

Do you regularly print full-page, full-bleed images or posters, or are miniature catalog shots your specialty? Together, the print dimensions of an image, the resolution of the final output device, and the screening technology used for output determine the appropriate image file size. The larger the anticipated print dimensions, the larger the files you'll need to prepare, and the more processing power you'll need to handle the job. But base your imaging system on the print dimensions of *typical* images, not on the occasional poster-size monster that comes your way.

Bus and Processor Speed

Although the central processing unit (CPU) of a computer isn't the only determinant of a system's speed, it's a major factor. If you typically output grayscale or small-format color images, a Macintosh Quadra (based on the Motorola 040 series chip) or a 486-based PC may meet your needs. But if high-volume imaging workloads, larger-format images, the use of HiFi color, or tight deadlines are your lot, consider a PowerPC system (Macintosh platform) or one based on the Intel Pentium (PC platform). PowerPCs are based on Motorola's 601 or 604 series *RISC* or *Reduced Instruction Set Computer* chips, which achieve high speeds by repeatedly building complex instructions out of simpler core instructions and by simultaneously executing multiple instructions. PowerPC and Pentium machines have the added advantage of being built around a *PCI* (*Peripheral Component Interconnect*) bus, whose 64-bit data highway for the management of all processing operations greatly improves throughput over older machines based on a 32-bit data highway. On the Macintosh platform, many companies specialize in providing Photoshop-specific accelerator boards. At the high end of the imaging market, throughput requirements dictate the use of a high-speed PowerPC or custom Macintosh-compatible workstation, Pentium, or UNIX-based workstation. (Witness the DayStar Genesis pictured in Figure 2–1.)

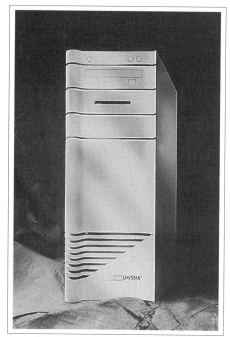

Figure 2–1   *courtesy DayStar Digital*

The DayStar Genesis MP, a high-end workstation running under the Macintosh operating system, features dual upgradable 120 MHz PowerPC processors for multiprocessing of complex tasks.

If you need to upgrade to meet prepress demands but can't afford to chuck your entire investment in an older machine, consider a new motherboard, a third-party accelerator board (Macintosh users), or a faster processor chip (PC users). Each approach has its advantages. Upgrading the motherboard gives you the best speed boost because you're upgrading the bus as well as the CPU. On the other hand, Macintosh professionals may have to invest in new RAM because a new motherboard doesn't accept your existing memory chips. If you buy a third-party CPU accelerator, you can

retain your existing RAM memory but may experience less than a maximum increase in speed because your bus and memory speeds are slower than those in a newer model computer.

System Memory (RAM)

For scanning and image processing tasks, having sufficient *RAM* (*random access memory*) is even more vital to system performance than having a fast CPU and bus. To run smoothly, many leading image-editing packages require an amount of RAM equal to several times the file size of the image you're currently working with (Photoshop uses three to five times the amount of image data in a file). If an image-editing program requests more RAM than you have available, it typically uses a scheme called *virtual memory*, which dips into your hard drive and uses its free space as pseudo RAM. Even the fastest hard drive is slower than RAM, so having to resort to virtual memory noticeably slows your system's performance. You're better off investing in extra memory for the sake of throughput.

A new generation of image-editing packages, which include Live Picture and Macromedia xRes, lets you manipulate hundreds of megabytes on a relatively low-memory diet, but even they have hefty memory requirements. Live Picture, which uses RAM to shuttle screen-sized *proxies* of the full image, still requires a minimum of 24MB, with 48MB recommended. Macromedia Xres requires 8MB. These amounts are above and beyond the amount of RAM needed to run your operating system and any other software you may have open at the same time!

Input

This category includes all the devices that bring images into your computer, or that enable you to view them accurately once they're in the system. Monitors and display adapters, hardware calibration devices, scanners, digital cameras, and CD-ROM drives all can contribute to or hinder your prepress productivity according to whether they match your imaging needs.

Display System

These days, having a 24-bit (16 million-color) color display adapter is *de rigueur* for imaging professionals, unless you work with grayscale images only. In a 32,000- or 64,000-color display, subtle tonal gradations may drop out that could make the difference between accurate color correction and manipulations that you regret once the color proofs have been run or the film output. And the dithering that takes place in a 256-color display system doesn't even come close to simulating accurate color. Simply having 24-bit color may not be enough since acceleration is also important if you have high-volume imaging requirements or work with multimegabyte files. On the Macintosh, there's a trend toward Photoshop-specific display acceleration, whereas acceleration on the Windows platform tends not to be restricted to a specific software package.

Monitor size is another important consideration for imaging professionals. For the sake of image-editing accuracy, it's vital to view an image at a 1:1 (actual size) ratio, yet most monitors display only 72 to 96 pixels per inch. The more data an image contains, the more time you're likely to spend scrolling the screen, especially with a smaller monitor. Consider a 17-inch monitor as the absolute minimum for imaging operations, and a 19- to 21-inch monitor as a better choice if you work with multi-megabyte color images.

Monitor Calibration Devices

Calibration—the process of obtaining consistent color representation between all system components in the production cycle—can be achieved through software aids, hardware devices, or both (see Chapter 4). If all your imaging projects have the same print parameters—for example, if you work exclusively on a monthly magazine, always output to the same proofing system and imagesetter, and always use the same press—then a basic software calibration utility such as Adobe Photoshop's Gamma may meet your needs for color accuracy. But for big-budget projects where color matching is critical, and for anyone having to deal with a wide variety of input sources and output parameters, a hardware-based luminance calibration device offers better calibration insurance. Calibration devices attach to a monitor's surface by suction and can be used to match output color to display color automatically with the help of software utilities, such as the ViewMatch calibration utility provided with ViewSonic monitors (Figure 2–2). The Light Source Colortron discussed in Chapter 4 is also handy for project-by-project color matching.

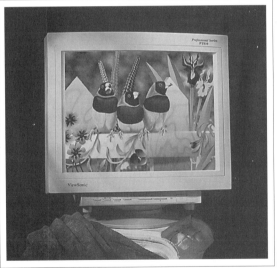

Figure 2–2

courtesy ViewSonic Corporation

This ViewSonic PT810, a flat-screen 21-inch monitor offering display resolutions up to 1,600 x 1,200 pixels, has a fine 0.30 mm aperture grille that produces vertical bars of color instead of dots for exceptionally bright, high-contrast images. The PT810 conforms to strict Swedish TCO standards, is cross-platform compatible, and is available with ViewMatch, a comprehensive monitor calibration system discussed in Chapter 4.

Note: *The stability of a monitor's phosphors is as important as having a luminance calibrator. Most monitors are unstable enough to require frequent recalibration during the working day in order to maintain strict accuracy. Stable CMOS-controlled reference monitors now coming onto the market reduce, if not eliminate, the necessity for display measurement.*

Scanners

While Chapter 1 focused on the technological factors that determine scanning quality, here we're concerned with what kind of scanner makes the best match for your print projects. Whether you use an in-house scanner to handle high-volume work or contract for the services of an outside vendor, you make the best use of your input dollar by employing a scanner that offers neither more nor less quality than you need. Here are some in-a-nutshell guidelines:

- **Drum scanners, high-bit flatbed, or film/transparency scanners**—High-end advertising and collateral, annual reports, critical scientific or technical applications, big-budget magazines, posters, fine-art reproductions, large-format color images

- **Film/transparency scanners**—Commercial-grade advertising and collateral, consumer and trade magazines, full-color catalogs, full-color and grayscale books (excepting fine-art books)

- **Midrange flatbed scanners**—Regionally distributed advertising, collateral, and catalogs; regional black-and-white periodicals (including newspapers); corporate communications documents; corporate manuals; one-color books

- **Low-end flatbed scanners**—Locally distributed flyers, in-house corporate communications, for-position-only images

Digital Cameras

For certain types of applications, digital cameras may offer a more convenient input solution than scanners. Here are some suggestions based on type of publication and budget:

- **Scan-back cameras**—Demanding scientific, medical, or technical applications, still product shots for big-budget catalogs

- **Higher-resolution array cameras**—Newspaper journalism, full-color catalogs containing medium- or small-format images, live-action photography

- **Low-resolution array cameras**—Small-format images for corporate journalism, low-budget catalogs containing small-format images, live-action photography

CD-ROM Drives

As the demand for Photo CD images grows among magazine, catalog, newspaper, and other print publishing professionals, so does the need for a CD-ROM drive fast enough to access and download images quickly. The deciding factor is the volume of images you must process. For the occasional user of Photo CD and stock photo images, a double-speed (2×) CD-ROM drive is adequate. For regular-use, high-volume applications, consider a 4×- or 6×-speed drive.

Tip: *For archiving publications, use a rewritable CD drive, which provides both input and storage in a single peripheral.*

Graphics Tablets

Pressure-sensitive drawing tablets like the example in Figure 2–3 are indispensable for creating original raster and vector artwork and compositing photomontages. Today's tablets are high-resolution—the pressure-sensitive pen can

Figure 2–3   *courtesy Wacom, Inc.*

The Wacom ArtZ II 6 x 8-inch graphics tablet includes a cordless, pressure-sensitive, "erasable" pen.

cover a large area of the monitor screen using only a small tablet surface area. Popular graphics tablet manufacturers include CalComp, Kurta, Summagraphics, and Wacom.

Image Storage

Everybody's going digital. Color files are on the increase. File size is on the increase. Add that up, and it's no wonder that image storage needs are ballooning at a rapid pace. Fortunately, storage options are diverse.

Internal Hard Drives

Hard drives may be adequate for day-to-day work, but once the project's over and ready for backup or long-term archival, other types of media are necessary. Even for short-term storage, hard-drive speed and capacity requirements are increasing as images continue to get bigger, hungrier, and more numerous.

Hard-drive speed is determined by seek time, access time, and transfer rate. *Seek time* measures how quickly the drive head can travel to the physical location on the track from which it

will read or to which it will write data. *Access time* is the amount of time needed for the drive data head to begin reading or writing data. *Transfer rate* refers to the amount of data that can pass back and forth between the computer and the hard drive in one second. High-capacity drives boast both the shortest seek times (8 ms or less) and the fastest transfer rates (4–5MB per second).

For networked imaging professionals (especially when large numbers of images and file sizes greater than 20MB are involved), a *disk array*, also known as a *RAID drive*, may be necessary to provide adequate speed. In a disk array setup, multiple high-speed drives are connected through a *SCSI* (Small Computer Systems Interface) controller and appear as a single-drive volume to your system. Data is written and read through multiple heads simultaneously, widening the effective data path and optimizing read/write times beyond what's possible with a single high-speed drive. Further levels of RAID use additional disks to provide backup by generating error-correction code that allows you to recover all data completely in the event that one drive fails.

Removable Drives

Removable magnetic hard drives have long been a standard—primarily for data transfer and secondarily for backup. (If you frequently transfer files to a service bureau or prepress house, SyQuest drives may be your most compatible option.) Drive mechanisms are easily affordable, and storage capacities continue to rise for SyQuest, Bernoulli, Zip, and PCMCIA data cartridges. Figure 2–4 depicts a high-capacity 270MB removable drive subsystem from SyQuest.

Removable drive cartridges do have some disadvantages. They're magnetic and so are more susceptible to damage and data loss than are optical cartridges. The lower-capacity drives

Figure 2–4   *courtesy SyQuest Int'l*

A SyQuest 270MB capacity removable drive system and cartridge

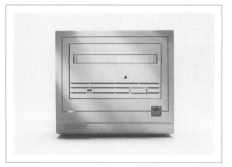

Figure 2–5   *courtesy Micronet*

The 1.3GB capacity MicroNet SB-TMO-1300 MO drive is fast enough to use for current work as well as archival. It features an access time of 18 ms and a sustained transfer rate of 2MB per second.

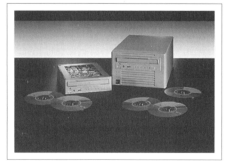

Figure 2–6   *courtesy Yamaha*

The Yamaha CDR 100 offers a quad-speed CD recording system, a quad-speed CD-ROM reader, and optical storage in a single drive.

are also much slower than hard drives, making them more suitable for archival than for current work. Finally, per-megabyte storage costs are generally higher for removable cartridges than for opticals. An exception is the Bernoulli Jaz, which offers throughput greater than 3MB per second and faster access times than magneto-optical drives.

Optical Drives

Rewritable magneto-optical, phase-change optical, and rewritable CD drives are rivaling removable magnetic drives as the new standards for high-volume, portable storage. They feature higher capacities, greater data reliability, and low per-megabyte storage cost.

Rewritable optical drives come in one of three basic types: magneto-optical, phase-change optical, or rewritable CD systems.

■ *Magneto-optical drives* (MO drives) are available in capacities of 128MB, 230MB, 600MB, 650MB, 1.3GB, 2.0GB, and 2.6GB. Drives with capacities below 660MB are best suited for backup and archival, since their access times and transfer rates are too low for use as work drives. However, higher-capacity 1.3, 2.0, and 2.6GB drives *can* be used for current projects, as their transfer speeds approach those of fast hard drives. Figure 2–5 depicts an example of a high-capacity 1.3GB MO drive. Multiple-drive *jukeboxes* are also commercially available for network servers.

■ *Phase-change optical drives*, unlike magneto-opticals, don't use any form of magnetism in either the drive or the disc media, so data is even more stable. Phase-change drives offer about 15 percent additional storage capacity per disc when compared with MO drives.

■ *Multifunction rewritable CD drives*, also based on phase-change technology, combine a double- or quad-speed CD-ROM reader with writable CD and optical storage functions. The media can store up to 650MB of data, making them ideal for multimedia and Photo CD development, as well as backup and data transfer. Plus, the versatility of multifunction drives reduces equipment clutter on your desktop. Figure 2–6 shows a quad-speed multifunction drive from Yamaha.

Tape Options

Tape drives and *DAT* (*digital audio tape*) drives remain popular, economical backup choices for single-user systems and networked servers, respectively. DAT drives can accommodate 2 to 10GB of storage per tape cartridge, which translates to just pennies per megabyte. But although tape backup may be cheap, it's not quite as data reliable or user friendly as some other types of mass storage. Tape can break or unravel, data transfer speeds are too slow to permit use as a work drive, and backup software must act as an intermediary to make file transfer possible. For high-volume imaging workloads, tape is also inconvenient. As files in a project change, you have to update the tape contents incrementally, saving the newest files in a separate volume rather than keeping all current project files together. And if you want to erase any old or outdated files on a tape, you have to erase the entire tape. Removable drives and opticals have no such limitations.

Digital Transmission

Modems are *de rigueur* for sending image or output files to a prepress house or service bureau and for exchanging data over the Internet with remote clients, vendors, or colleagues. Since image and PostScript output files are among the largest you'll ever squeeze through a telephone line, it pays to use a modem with a minimum baud rate of 14,400 bps (bits per second), and preferably one rated at 28,800 bps.

Sometimes overnight shipment to a client, designer, prepress house, or print vendor isn't fast enough. If you're in a field such as advertising or periodical publishing, where constant communications, last-minute changes, and high-volume data transfers are the norm, consider setting up a special communications line

called an *ISDN connection*. ISDN lines are all-digital and, therefore, free from the static disturbances to which normal telephone lines are subject. The setup cost of installing the copper-based line for a home or residentially based business is only about a hundred dollars, and usage fees average only about $25 per month. With ISDN, a 5MB file can be transferred to its destination in a single minute.

Software Solutions

The speediest, most expensive hardware peripherals in the imaging world exist only to serve and exploit the potentials of powerful software. In this section of the chapter, we survey software essentials for imaging professionals who work in print publishing fields. Since this book is about production, we'll focus on software that assists output-related tasks rather than creative ones. We'll also make recommendations based on task-oriented considerations such as the types of documents you print, typical image file size, and volume of work.

Image-Editing, Paint, and Compositing Software

The lines between designers, communicators, illustrators, and production professionals are blurred at best. These days, it's not unusual for one person (or one department) to conceptualize, execute, and output a raster illustration, so professional-level imaging software must encompass both the creative and production aspects of a job. In this book, we focus on production-related tasks, but many software packages offer both creative and production-oriented controls. Among image-editing packages, the standouts include the bi-platform Adobe Photoshop and Macromedia xRes; Live Picture on the Macintosh; and Micrografx

Picture Publisher on the PC. Both xRes and Live Picture are geared toward users who must manipulate extremely large image files without sacrificing image-processing speed. Notable image-creation applications include Fractal Design Painter (which runs on both platforms) and Corel PhotoPAINT! under Windows.

Macromedia xRes

Macromedia xRes works by *selective processing*—applying commands only to the pixels visible at the current magnification level until it's time to render the perfected image. Requiring only 8MB of RAM and offering identical versions on both the Macintosh and Windows platforms, xRes includes tools similar to Photoshop's. Like Photoshop, xRes provides the convenience of layering and channel operations. In addition, it emphasizes creative manipulation tools (such as natural-media brushes), much like a high-end paint program.

Live Picture

The Macintosh-based Live Picture (from the company of the same name) permits real-time editing of even the largest image files, thanks to the FITS technology that stores all edits as a series of mathematical commands, then applies them to and renders the final image when the composition is complete. Images are truly resolution independent—only at rendering time do you specify output dimensions and file size. LivePicture is especially strong in its implementation of retouching, compositing, layering, perspective, and batch processing controls.

Filters

Adobe's introduction of a standard for the creation of modular *plug-in* filters several years ago has spawned a burgeoning aftermarket of products that can be used with any image-editing package that supports the standard.

Although many third-party filters aim at artistic or special effects, a good many are useful as scanning, production, and processing tools. Here's a brief rundown of some of the more useful production filters, some of which we'll discuss in other chapters:

- CD/Q and CD/Q Batch (Human Software) perform prepress enhancement and color separations of Photo CD images as they are being accessed and downloaded.

- FotoMagic (Ring of Fire) is a series of specialized color-correction and enhancement filters that mimic high-end darkroom techniques.

- Intellihance Pro (DPA Software) applies intelligent, automated processing to grayscale, RGB, or CMYK images and prepares color separations based on sets of user-defined preferences.

- PhotoImpress (Display Technologies) provides speedy on-the-fly enhancement and separations for Photo CD images.

- PlateMaker (IN Software) permits color separation into more than four plates, which is useful for spot colors, foil stamping, varnishes, HiFi color, and so on.

- PhotoSpot (Second Glance Software) is a series of color-separation filters that uses color-reduction technology to generate high-quality spot color separations from low-resolution printers.

- PrintCal PI (Candela) calibrates multiple color printers and proofers, making it useful in a service bureau, advertising, or color prepress setting.

- ScanPrepPro (ImageXpress, Inc.) automates scanner setup for the desired output result and provides enhancement and color separations using artificial intelligence.

- Spectre filters (PrePress Technologies) offer sophisticated color-correction and unsharp masking capabilities.

Tip: *Some special-effects filters also have their uses in a production context. For example, noise filters can help obliterate halftone screening patterns in scans of previously printed originals.*

Color Management Systems

If calibration ensures color compatibility between components in a single system, *color management* addresses the wider issue of defining the color characteristics of any device in a standardized way, so that color can be transferred consistently from any device on any system to any other device, anywhere. Current color management systems (CMS) software follows two distinct trends: color management at the operating system level—ColorSync 2 on the Macintosh and Image Color Matching (ICM) under Windows 95—and stand-alone software packages such as Agfa FotoTune, EfiColor Works, and the myriad Kodak CMS products.

Do you really need CMS software? You *don't* if you always derive images from the same input source, always edit them on the same monitor and output them to the same device(s), and manually calibrate each input and output component on a regular basis. You *do* need a CMS if more than one of the following conditions apply:

- Your source images come from a variety of input devices, or from multiple designers, clients, or vendors whose input methods you can't control.
- Images are edited on multiple monitors by more than one manufacturer.
- You use various color proofing devices.
- Your publications are of different types and are output on more than one type of press or use more than one paper stock.

CMSs aren't a panacea for image production problems. After all, for most images you should be concerned with emphasizing the intended message of an image rather than with slavishly matching input color to output color. But when the production workflow dictates the involvement of many people and devices, a CMS can help. Chapter 4 surveys important CMS options.

Productivity Software

"Do it faster. Do it smarter. Do more of it, more efficiently. Get organized!" If little gremlins on your shoulder whisper messages like these into your ear, you owe it to your sanity to investigate specialized software packages and plug-ins that can make the gremlins go away. What we like to call "productivity software" comes in three distinct flavors.

- *Image management* or *image database* software allows you to organize large numbers of images by subject, project, or any category to which you can attach a keyword. It's especially useful for cataloging the contents of a project or images that may need to be reused in a variety of projects over time. Adobe Fetch, Kudo Image Browser, and U–Lead Image Pals are examples of popular image database packages.

- *Intelligent processing* software uses artificial intelligence to perform all the steps involved in preparing an image for print in one sweep. Typically, you can save and load multiple sets of parameters, swapping them out according to the output requirements of the current image. CD/Q (Human Software), DPA Intellihance, and ScanPrepPro from ImageXPress allow you to automate prepress operations, one image at a time.

- *Batch processing* software takes artificial intelligence one step further, allowing you to apply scripts or sets of steps to whole groups of images. CD/Q Batch, PhotoImpress (Display Technologies), PhotoMatic (DayStar/Kodak), and Equilibrium DeBabelizer are good examples.

Page Composition Software

Odds are, the images you prepare for print output are part of a larger document that includes text and other graphics composed in QuarkXpress, Adobe PageMaker, or Adobe FrameMaker. If you produce many such documents—especially if you frequently use the output services of a color prepress house or service bureau—it pays to work with an industry-standard page layout package that your service vendor already knows intimately. Output service vendors tend to specialize in one or two programs and in the utilities designed to optimize output from those programs. If you use a package with whose foibles the vendor is not famliar, you may either have to create your own PostScript output files (with little assistance) or cross your fingers, knowing that the vendor may be able to do little to troubleshoot any output problems that arise. The best strategy is to locate a quality service vendor, build a relationship with that vendor, then base your choice of page composition software on the vendor's special expertise. That way, you'll get the support you need to complete every project successfully.

Output and Proofing Devices

With color images, it's especially important to see a *proof* (test print) of the composite image before consigning the files to an imagesetter or platesetter for color separations. Proofing devices vary widely in the accuracy and quality of their color reproduction and in the amount of information they provide. Ideally, you should obtain proofs more than once during the production cycle. In the design phase, you can use low-cost color proofs from inkjet, thermal wax transfer, and color laser printers to check approximate image color and overall

color balance. These devices, while affordable for small-scale publishing enterprises, corporate communications groups, and independent design studios, don't deliver the kind of resolution or color accuracy to ensure that things will turn out WYSIWYG in print. Neither do they provide indications of potential press-related problems such as dot gain, trapping, or moiré.

That's why it's necessary to obtain more sophisticated types of color proofs later, as you prepare to output color separations to film or plate. Digital proofs (high-end inkjet or dye sublimation—see Figure 2–7), overlay and laminate proofs created from film separations, and press proofs made using the actual paper and inks scheduled for the press run provide industry-standard levels of color accuracy. Overlay and laminate proofs are also able to show up potential trapping, halftone dot structure, and dot gain errors so that you can accurately compensate for suspected problems before incurring the expense of final output and printing. Chapter 4 contains more information about color proofing devices.

Figure 2–7   *courtesy Fargo Electronics*

The 600 x 300 dpi Fargo Primera Pro can generate both thermal wax transfer and photorealistic dye sublimation color prints, making it an economical choice for designers who need to generate color proofs at multiple stages of the production process. It supports PostScript Level 2 on both the Macintosh and Windows platforms.

Screening and Print Reproduction Basics

3

The images you edit on your monitor are *continuous tone*, showing smooth transitions between adjacent colors or shades of gray. To a printing press, however, a dot of ink is an all-or-nothing proposition—it's either there or it isn't, and it's always the same solid color. Yet, for large quantities, the per-unit cost is far lower when using offset lithography than when using devices such as dye sublimation, thermal wax transfer, and inkjet printers. The challenge of print reproduction is, therefore, one of how to simulate hundreds of gray shades using a single color (black) or millions of colors using only four colors (cyan, magenta, yellow, and black).

Two different technological approaches to this problem have developed over the past decade. *Digital halftoning*, which is still the mainstream approach, grew out of a traditional process of photographing a subject through a grid of a certain frequency in order to convert it to a pattern of variably sized dots. Black-and-white laser printers, most color laser printers, and PostScript-based imagesetters and platemakers are considered *halftoning devices*

25

because they typically use this technology to generate output. *Frequency-modulated (FM) screening*, a rival newcomer, does away with patterning entirely, using a mathematically derived method for placing fixed-sized dots at what seem to be random locations. Multiple implementations of both methods exist. In this chapter, we'll provide a solid understanding of digital halftoning and FM screening and explore their implications for how you can best prepare images for the printing process.

Digital Halftoning Basics

The object of halftoning is to make itself invisible. When executed correctly, digital halftoning creates the optical illusion of continuous tone. Halftoning achieves this illusion through *amplitude-moderated (AM) screening*, a method by which variably sized dots are arranged on a regular grid, with the centers of the dots spaced equidistant from one another (Figure 3–1). We perceive larger dots as darker tones and smaller dots as lighter ones.

A halftone screen has three components: frequency, dot shape, and angle. Each component makes a different contribution to the quality of a printed image.

Original

Variably sized, evenly spaced halftone dots

© Emil Ihrig

Figure 3–1

In halftone (AM) screening, the sizes of the dots vary to simulate different tones, while the distance between them remains fixed.

Screen Frequency, Tonal Range, and Detail

The *screen frequency* or *line screen* that you specify for final output in an image-editing or page layout package dictates the fineness of the halftone grid and, consequently, the apparent level of detail in the image. Screen frequency is measured in *lines per inch (lpi)*. As Figure 3–2 shows, the amount of visible detail increases as screen frequency increases. Prepress professionals often state that higher line screens make an image sharper, but they don't mean more in focus; they're simply expressing the fact that at higher screen frequencies, more of the *available* detail can be reproduced.

Tip: *Press type and paper stock characteristics limit the highest screen frequency that can be used effectively. For example, if you specify a 175 lpi screen, but the press can handle only a 150 lpi screen, printing at the higher frequency will only result in reduced contrast, loss of detail in the shadows, and an apparent increase in dot gain. If a print vendor suggests one of two maximum screen frequencies, use the lower of the two for the clearest, crispest detail in print.*

Screen frequency and printer resolution also have a bearing on the printable *tonal range*—the number of discrete tones that can be expressed accurately between solid black and paper white. Granted, printed materials have inherently lower densities than film-based

20 lpi   65 lpi   133 lpi   © Emil Ihrig

Figure 3–2

The amount of detail that can be reproduced by a halftoning output device is determined by the halftone screen frequency, or number of halftone dots per linear inch. Detail increases with screen frequency.

photographic originals—compare the 1.5 to 2.0 dynamic range typical of press prints with the 2.8 to 3.2 range typical of color slides. But a line screen above 150 lpi *can* optimize the tonal range that a press print can achieve, as long as the following three conditions apply:

- The image already has a broad tonal range due to the way it was input.
- The resolution of the final output device is high enough to support a full 256 tonal levels per color channel.
- The press type and paper stock can successfully hold the dot at higher line screens.

Press setup, document type, and print run are the factors that customarily determine the screen frequency to be used for a particular job. Table 3–1 lists the screen frequencies typically assigned to various types of printed documents. Take these suggestions with a grain of salt and consult your print or prepress vendor for recommended specifications.

Note: *Documents requiring high-volume print runs are often printed using a rotogravure or flexographic press rather than offset press. These press types use printing plates that are heavy and durable enough to withstand the reproduction of hundreds of thousands or even millions of copies.*

Note: *Higher lpi doesn't improve poor-quality originals, it merely exposes them. The actual detail delivered by any halftone is limited to the quality of the detail in the digital image.*

Halftone Cells, Spots, and Dots

Digital halftoning devices such as laser printers and imagesetters can create only fixed-sized dots (let's call them *spots* to avoid confusing them with halftone dots). To simulate variably sized halftone dots, these devices group the fixed-sized spots together in a matrix called a

Document Type	Press Setup	Screen Frequency Range (lpi)
High-end advertising; high-end brochures and annual reports; fine art books, fine art reproductions	Sheet-fed/coated	150 to 300
Newsletters, forms, flyers	Sheet-fed/uncoated	100 to 133
Consumer and trade magazines; commercial-grade advertising and collateral; catalogs	Heat set web/coated	100 to 150
Smaller circulation magazines; catalogs; direct-mail pieces; most long-run, medium-quality print jobs	Heat set web/uncoated	90 to 133
Quality Sunday supplements	Newspaper/coated	65 to 100
Low-quality Sunday supplements	Newspaper/uncoated	65 to 100
Newspapers, pulp catalogs	Newspaper/newsprint	65 to 100

Table 3–1

Typical Recommended Screen Frequency Settings Based on Press Setup and Document Type

halftone cell (Figure 3–3). The number of *potential* shades that a given halftone cell can reproduce depends on both the screen frequency and the resolution of the output device (see the "Contrast Versus Detail: Printer Resolution and Screen Frequency" section following), but an individual halftone cell reproduces only one shade of gray or one shade of a process ink color. The density of that shade and the size of the halftone dot are directly related to the number of fixed-sized spots in each halftone cell, which in turn is determined by the numeric tonal value (0 to 255) assessed for each pixel.

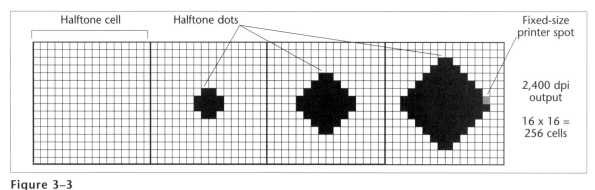

Figure 3–3

As the number of fixed-sized printer spots in a digital halftone cell increases, so does the apparent density or darkness of the tone.

Contrast Versus Detail: Printer Resolution and Screen Frequency

Ideally, a printed grayscale image should be able to reproduce 256 shades of gray, and a full-color image should be able to reproduce 256 shades for each of the process ink colors. However, the number of possible shades that a halftone cell can express is limited by the resolution of the printing device (its *spot size* or dot size determines how many dots fit into each horizontal inch). In fact, the relationship between printer resolution and halftone screen frequency is an inverse one. Here's how to calculate the maximum number of shades per color that a given device can reproduce using digital halftoning:

```
(Printer resolution ÷ Halftone screen frequency)² + 1
           = Maximum number of tonal levels
```

You can understand why digital halftoning works this way if you recall that a printer's linear resolution is fixed. As you cram additional halftone dots into each linear inch, fewer spots are available to each horizontal grid line in a halftone cell. As the line screen increases, the number of potential gray shades that each halftone cell can reproduce decreases geometrically. A 300 dpi laser printer, for example, can reproduce no more than 33 shades of gray at a line screen of 53 lpi ([300 ÷ 53]² + 1 = approximately 33). If you crank up the line screen to 75 lpi, you get more detail, but tonal range is compressed and the image is higher in contrast because the halftone cells can't express as many discrete tones ([300 ÷ 75]² + 1 = 17). By the same reasoning, a 600 dpi printer can reproduce 65 tones at a screen frequency of 75 lpi, and a 1,200 dpi printer or imagesetter can reproduce 145 tones at a screen frequency of 100 lpi. An imagesetter or platesetter printing at 2,400 dpi can reproduce the full PostScript-determined range of 256 tones per color at line screens of up to 150 lpi.

Dot Shape

A second component of digital halftone screens is the shape of the halftone dot. At extremely low screen frequencies (10 to 30 lpi), dot shape is easy to perceive (Figure 3–4), but at higher frequencies it becomes progressively less obvious to the naked eye.

(a) Original, 133 lpi

(b) Diamond, 15 lpi

(c) Ellipse, 15 lpi

(d) Line, 15 lpi   © Emil Ihrig

Figure 3–4

If halftone dot shape is chosen so as not to distract from the subject matter of a picture (a), it is obvious to the naked eye only at very low halftone screen frequencies (b, c, d).

Dot shape should subtly enhance the content of an image, not distract from it. Choose a shape that harmonizes with the shapes in the main subjects and the tonal distribution of the image. Image-editing and page layout packages offer quite a multitude of dot shapes for halftoning—round, square, elliptical, line, diamond, cross, and so on. Round dots are often used for product shots, elliptical dots for human subjects, and square dots for subjects that require crisp definition. Round or elliptical dots are usually the best types to assign for black-and-white printing; elliptical dots work best for color printing. Consult your print and prepress vendors for guidance on the shapes to use for specific images.

Caution: *Elliptical dots print properly only when the* blankets—*the part of the press that contacts and imprints the paper—are kept clean. Otherwise, the dots may plug up on press.*

Tip: *Most page layout packages let you assign only one group of halftone screen settings to all the images in a document (QuarkXPress is one exception—it allows you to customize screening on an image-by-image basis, but only for grayscale and black-and-white images). There may be times, though, when you want certain images to have dot shape, screen frequency, or screen angle attributes that differ from the rest of the images in the layout. A good workaround strategy is to save the "variant" images as EPS files in your image-editing package, making sure to embed the desired halftone screen settings in each file so that they can't be overwritten by the final printer or imagesetter. Be sure to test the results before press time on the imagesetter you will actually use for the job, though. Some imagesetter RIPs don't recognize custom screens and, instead, run the images at the imagesetter default screen.*

Screen Angle, Patterning, and Output Resolution

Screen angles, more than any other component of halftone screening, determine whether the optical illusion of halftone patterning is inconspicuous or unpleasantly obvious to the eye. Angles also impact the amount of data that an image needs to contain in order to output well. Let's examine the whys and wherefores of screen angles and their implications for printing your digital images.

Why Screen Angles?

Screen patterning for digitally halftoned images always prints at an angle. For grayscale images, the default angle is 45 degrees. For full-color images, the four CMYK plates are offset from each other at different angles, traditionally 105 degrees for cyan, 75 degrees for magenta, 90 or 0 degrees for yellow, and 45 degrees for black (see Figure C–2 in the Color Gallery). When printing plates align properly, the four colors come together to form small rose-shaped clusters of dots called *rosettes*. The rationale behind these traditional angles derives partly from the way the human eye perceives angles, partly from observations about the relative prominence of colors to our vision, and partly from the way inks of different colors interact with paper on press.

- **Angles and visual perception**—The human eye quickly spots an angle that's perfectly aligned with the horizontal or vertical plane (0 or 90 degrees, respectively). A perfect diagonal (45 degrees) is halfway between the two and therefore offers the least obtrusive compromise. This explains why screens for grayscale images and the black plate for CMYK images typically print at 45 degrees.

Tip: *There's one important exception to the rule about outputting grayscales at a 45-degree angle. If the content of an image emphasizes diagonal lines, a 45-degree angle might produce rough interference patterns or draw attention to itself and should be avoided.*

- **Angles for specific colors**—The relative darkness or lightness of the CMYK colors determines how far each screen should be offset from a perfectly horizontal or vertical angle. Black is the darkest and so is screened at the maximum distance from these "no-no" angles. Cyan and magenta screens are both offset 15 degrees from the vertical, but in opposite directions. As the lightest color, yellow can safely be screened at a perfectly horizontal or vertical angle without making itself obvious.

Tip: *If the subject matter of an image contains large amounts of intense yellow, swap the yellow angle with that of another color and then feel free to emphasize the yellow.*

- **Angles and overprinting**—If inks were applied to all screens at the same angle on press, colors would muddy tremendously and dot gain—the spreading of ink dots that contributes to making colors look darker on paper than they do on your monitor—would be an even bigger headache than it is already. Offsetting the screens for each color keeps the composite result looking crisp—provided it works smoothly.

Provided it works smoothly—that's the sore point for managing screen angles in digital halftoning. Any number of factors, from image content to the use of previously scanned images to misalignment of plates during output or printing, can conspire to turn inconspicuous rosettes into blatantly obvious patterns. Let's look at some of the causes of these mishaps and the solutions that software screening developers have contrived to work around them.

Screen Angle Pitfalls and Solutions

Moirés—annoyingly visible halftone screen patterning that distracts the viewer from the image's message—are among the worst nightmares of every designer, color separator, and press operator. Screen angles that produce out-of-control dot shapes are the culprit usually responsible for moirés, but their causes can vary widely. For example:

- *Content moirés* come about when an image contains regular patterning that interferes with screen patterning, such as fabric or a digitally derived texture. Adjusting angles of the offending colors can sometimes help, as well as can the application of certain filters discussed in Chapter 10.

- *Misregistration*, or improper alignment of color plates, is another big offender. Misregistration can occur either during output when a screen angle slightly different from what was requested is delivered, or on press where moirés result because rosettes go out of synchronization. Newer imagesetter and platesetter screening technologies have virtually eliminated the PostScript-induced moirés that can occur during output.

- *Reprinting previously halftoned originals* is a third common cause of moirés. Previously printed originals already contain halftone patterning, which interferes with the new patterning applied on top of it. You usually can compensate for or eliminate existing halftone patterning either during the scanning process or in an image-editing package (see Chapter 10).

Even if none of these problematic conditions apply, it's still possible to incur moirés in print because of output device limitations. The grids created by imagesetters and platesetters during halftone processing consist of square pixels, which easily match the 45- and 90-degree angles of the black and yellow plates but don't align consistently with the traditional 105- and 75-degree angles of cyan and magenta. The challenge is then to find angles for the cyan and magenta plates that both fit the imagesetter's pixel grid *and* still allow the halftone dots for all four plates to synchronize with each other to create a perfect rosette.

Happily, imagesetter and color separation software developers have devised several types of workarounds to this inherent glitch in the digital halftoning process. One approach involves increasing or reducing the requested screen frequency slightly through software to find a perfect match for all four plates using the traditional angles. This strategy reduces the risk of moiré but can reduce image quality slightly due to the output resolution not matching the screen frequency (see "Screen Angles, Frequency, and Output Resolution," following). Most PostScript screening technologies follow a *rational tangent screening* approach, which rounds off the cyan and magenta angles to the nearest angle that matches the imagesetter grid at a given output resolution. However, these angles are often far from the traditional angles and can sometimes alter the screen frequency, resulting in moirés. Some imagesetter manufacturers take this strategy one step further, basing halftone screens on supercells made up of a matrix of multiple halftone cells. Each supercell intersects the imagesetter's grid consistently, allowing for angles that more approximate the traditional ones. Today, high-end, proprietary systems such as Scitex and major imagesetter manufacturers use a compute-intensive process called *irrational screening*, which calculates the placement of each halftone dot individually rather than automatically based on a grid.

Out of this continuing search for a foolproof answer to the screen angle conundrum, a new class of screening technologies called *frequency-modulated* (FM) *screening* has arisen. See the "FM Screening Alternatives" section of this chapter for more information about the advantages of FM screening over digital halftoning and the new challenges it presents to quality print reproduction. First, though, let's take a look at the role that halftone screen angles play in determining how much data an image should contain.

Screen Angles, Frequency, and Output Resolution

The resolution at which an image should be sent to the final output device is called the *output resolution*, and it is determined by the halftone screen frequency—or so they say. The oft-quoted rule of thumb in the digital prepress industry is that output resolution should equal two times the screen frequency (300 ppi for a 150-line screen, for example). In actuality, screen frequency *and* screen angles determine how much data an image should contain, and for most types of images, the ideal output resolution-to-screen-frequency ratio, also known as the *halftoning factor* or *quality factor*, is much closer to 1.5:1 than 2:1.

> **❝The ideal halftoning factor is much closer to 1.5:1 than 2:1.❞**

Here's why. Input resolution, whether from a scanner or digital camera, is always measured at a horizontal angle of zero degrees. But when an imagesetter, platesetter, or other PostScript output device generates digital halftones or color separations, the halftone screens are rotated at an angle so that the observer's eye doesn't perceive the screen patterning. The most important thing to remember is that of the four CMYK screen angles, the 45-degree angle of the black plate represents the widest angle relative to a horizontal line.

This discrepancy between the perfectly horizontal angle of scanning resolution and the angles of halftone screens is important because it impacts the amount of information necessary to build each halftone dot in PostScript. Theoretically, a single pixel should provide all the information necessary to generate one halftone dot—a perfect 1:1 ratio. In practice, this doesn't happen, because when you rotate a horizontal line of a given length by 45 degrees, the *horizontal* real estate it covers is greatly diminished (see Figure 3–5). To compensate for that apparent "shortening," you'd have to extend the horizontal line by 1.41 times its original length, equaling the length of the diagonal line. Note also that in the halftone

diagram in Figure 3–5, a right triangle is formed by the horizontal line (B, the scanner CCD array), the vertical line (A, scanner CCD travel), and the diagonal line (C, the direction of the halftone dot). Remember the $A^2 + B^2 = C^2$ right triangle geometry equation you learned in high school? That's just another way of saying that the diagonal line—the line that represents the halftone screen angle—is 1.41 times longer than either the horizontal or the vertical line.

Note: *We have the ancient Greeks to thank for the "square root of 2" solution. They devised this halftoning rule while the angles of the Parthenon were only a glint in Pythagoras' eye.*

What this means is that the raster image processor (RIP) of a PostScript halftoning device requires the equivalent of only about 1.41 pixels of data to produce one accurate halftone dot—not two pixels as is often assumed. (The ratios would be even lower than 1.4:1 for the cyan, magenta, and yellow angles, which are less distant from the horizontal or vertical plane. But 1.41:1 takes care of the worst-case scenario black angle.)

The case becomes even clearer when you recognize that a RIP averages *all* the tonal values within each halftone cell area to arrive at a single number from which it can produce one halftone dot. Figure 3–6 shows that if an image contains much more information than necessary (2:1 output resolution-to-screen-frequency ratio), then the RIP ends up averaging multiple color or grayscale values and reducing them to a single value, with unfortunate consequences for image contrast and detail.

The moral of the story is that more isn't better; it's simply more. Cramming more data into an image file only increases storage and output costs and doesn't benefit the quality of the printed version; in fact, output quality may be compromised. In most cases, a halftoning

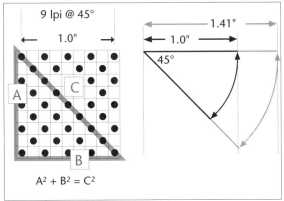

Figure 3–5

courtesy ImageXpress, Inc.

*Why a 1.41:1 output resolution-to-screen-frequency ratio makes sense. Rotating a horizontal line by 45 degrees (**right**), which occurs in the halftone screen of the black printing plate (**left**), results in an apparent "shortening" of the horizontal area covered by the rotated line (**right**). Increasing the line length by a factor of 1.41 compensates for this shortening effect. Basic geometry shows that the 45-degree angle of the black plate (the widest CMYK angle relative to the horizontal plane) generates a line 1.41 times longer than the horizontal line that represents the angle of scanning.*

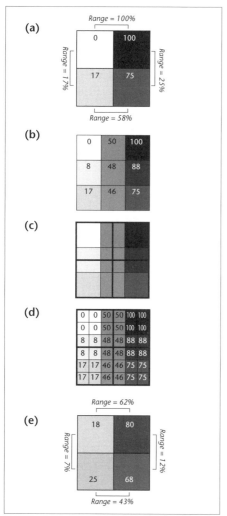

Figure 3–6

courtesy ImageXPress, Inc.

Including excess pixels in an image can result in a loss of contrast and detail after halftoning. (a) Adjacent pixel values before halftoning in an image with a 1.4:1 ppi-to-lpi ratio. (b) Adjacent pixel values before halftoning in an image with a 2:1 ppi-to-lpi ratio. (c) The imagesetter's RIP averages all values in a halftone cell to derive one value per halftone dot. (d) The RIP adds all tone values in each cell and divides them by the number of cell components (here, nine). (e) The result of this averaging process is reduced contrast and detail compared with the version before halftoning (b) or with an image that contains just the right amount of data (a).

factor of 1.5 is sufficient to reproduce optimum detail and contrast. The only exceptions to this rule may be extremely detailed images such as architectural drawings.

FM Screening Alternatives

As you've seen, screen angles and the necessity of maintaining exact, regular patterning are stumbling blocks that often prevent digital halftoning from maintaining the optical illusion of continuous tone in print. The search for workable solutions has led to the emergence of a relatively new technology, *frequency-modulated* or *FM screening*, which is rapidly growing in popularity as a viable real-world alternative to halftone screening.

Whereas halftone screening represents tones by using variably sized dots spaced evenly on a grid, FM screening uses fixed-sized dots (or, in some stochastic screening implementations, variably sized dots) spaced at *random* intervals (see Figure C–3 in the Color Gallery). This apparently random method of dot placement, which is actually the result of mathematical algorithms, effectively does away with recognizable patterning and the moiré problems that plague such patterning. Areas that contain a higher density of dots appear darker, while areas that contain a sparser number of dots are perceived as lighter. The dots used in FM screening are also far smaller than the dots used in halftoning, typically ranging between 15 and 40 microns—a 19-micron FM dot is equivalent to a halftoned 1 percent highlight dot at a 150 lpi! Notice the differences in dot sizes and patterning in the AM- and FM-screened versions of the rose in Figure 3–7.

In FM screening, there's no meaningful screen frequency because there's no regular screen pattern. What counts is the resolution of the output device and the smallest-sized halftone dot that a given press can hold at a comparable halftone screen frequency. Together, these factors determine the sizes of the FM dots to be used for most implementations. The higher the imagesetter or platesetter resolution, the smaller the size of the tiniest dot that can be used and the more finely detail can be rendered.

FM screening offers several advantages over digital halftoning, but it also presents new challenges to print

AM-screening, 133 lpi

300% zoom

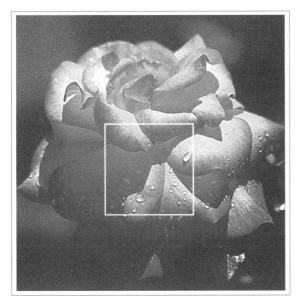

FM-screening, 41-micron dot (635 dpi FM resolution)

300% zoom

© Emil Ihrig

Figure 3–7

*Halftoning produces variably sized dots spaced at even intervals (**top**); FM screening features extremely tiny fixed- or variably-sized dots spaced at variable intervals (**bottom**). FM screening's superior detail rendering can be advantageous for documents printed on coated stocks with high ink coverage limits. The stand-alone Icefields application from Isis Imaging Corp. was used to generate the FM-screened version of the image.*

quality. Let's briefly survey the benefits and disadvantages of FM screening technologies.

FM Screening Advantages

Young as the technology is, FM screening already offers potent benefits for some high-end printing applications, particularly when images feature high-bit color, broad dynamic ranges with smooth tonal transitions, and intricate detail. Here's how and why:

- **Cleaner colors**—With the dangers of moiré eliminated, colors are more crisply defined and less subject to mutual contamination.

- **Improved edge definition and detail**—An *edge* occurs wherever there's contrast between two adjacent pixels. The small dot sizes used in FM screening contribute to sharp edge delineations and detail rendering in all tonal ranges, but especially in highlights and shadows. FM's superior edge definition characteristics make it ideal for reproducing fine details in fabrics and jewelry.

- **Smooth gradations between adjacent tones**—Subjects that show subtle, continuous gradations in shading are often rendered more smoothly by FM screening than through digital halftoning, provided that the implementation you use corrects for the noise that's often observable in low-contrast areas of an image.

- **Printing more than four colors**—Printing more than four plates can be a tricky proposition with halftoned screens because the odds of misregistration increase with every color that's added. FM screening has shown high tolerance for misregistration, which makes it ideal for printing images that require extra plates for spot varnishes, fluorescent inks, metallic colors, or what has come to be known as HiFi color (see Chapter 4).

- **Lower scan and output resolutions**—Many users contend that at a given nominal

screen frequency, FM screening requires less image data than digital halftoning to create high-quality output. Some say the quality factor is as low as 1:1 for FM screening, compared with 1.5:1 for halftoning. This would mean that an image to be output at a nominal screen ruling of 150 lpi could deliver excellent FM-screened results using an output resolution of only 150 ppi, but that a resolution of 225 ppi would be necessary to obtain the same level of quality for a halftoned version of the image. Less image data passing through the imagesetter's RIP translates to faster throughput and eventual output cost savings as the technology matures. Another option would be to retain the same amount of data in an image as if you were halftoning it, but then to output it at a higher nominal line screen using FM screening.

Tip: Not everyone agrees that users of FM screening should use lower scan and output resolutions. Professionals at the high end of the print market feel that since FM screening can render detail even better than halftone screening, it's to your advantage to use output resolutions that are equal to or higher than what you would use for halftoning. You're most likely to benefit from FM's potential advantages for high-resolution images if you will be printing on coated stocks with a sheet-fed press.

FM Screening Challenges

For all its potential benefits, FM screening still needs to have a few kinks worked out of it. Some software-based solutions to the perceived problems already exist; others are under development. The amount of experience a print or prepress vendor has had with the technology also makes a difference in the quality of the results you obtain. Here are some of the potential pitfalls:

- **Dot gain**—Dot gain describes the tendency of halftone dots to spread when ink is applied on press. Dot gain ranges for conventionally halftoned images fall between 18 and 25 percent according to *SWOP* (*Standard Web Offset Printing*) specifications. But FM-screened images are subject to exceptionally heavy dot gain—25 to 35 percent on coated stock, and up to 50 percent on uncoated stock. This happens because even though the FM dots are tiny, they have more absolute surface area around them in which to spread. The dot gain challenge isn't insurmountable, though. FM screening vendors who are also imagesetter or platesetter manufacturers supply software-based *transfer curves* for their equipment to precompensate for the anticipated dot gain. Transfer curves are similar to the curves you use to adjust tone and color in a digital image, except that they alter the way the imagesetter itself reproduces tones. If the imagesetter or platesetter that creates the output is *linearized* (calibrated for stability), and if the proper precompensation curve is applied during output, dot gain need not be a problem.

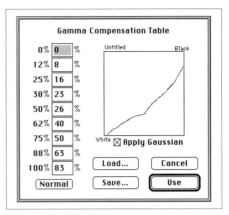

Figure 3–8

Icefields from Isis Imaging Corp., a device-independent FM screening application for the Macintosh platform, lets you output FM-screened and halftoned images together on the same page. Users can create custom transfer curves to precompensate for dot gain.

- **Graininess**—Some end users of FM screening technologies have observed graininess in low-contrast areas of the final printed images. A few FM software developers, including R.R. Donnelley & Sons, have added capabilities for isolating and removing noise; ask about this feature when specifying a job for FM screening. If noise isolation isn't an option, consider outputting to a system that permits both kinds of screening within the same document so that you can prepare low-contrast images for digital halftoning and other images for FM screening. Screen USA FM screening products, for example, allow halftoning and FM screening for different portions of the same image, while the stand-alone application Icefields (Figure 3–8) lets you select individual images on any page for FM screening.

Tip: To avoid graininess when all the images in a document are low in contrast, use digital halftone screening instead of FM screening.

- **Too-small dot sizes**—Imagesetter manufacturers' FM screening solutions typically allow only one or two fixed dot sizes at a given output resolution, and these are generally too small for use on uncoated and newspaper stocks or in screen printing, where dot gain is harder to control. The tiny dot sizes are also partly responsible for the noise observed in low-contrast images. The trend now is toward more flexible choices for each output resolution and dot sizes up to 100 microns (as compared with only 30 to 40 microns previously).

- **Quality control**—Due to the dot gain issue, FM-screened output tends to be unforgiving of dusty work environments, unlinearized imagesetters, and careless handling. The best solution is to work with prepress houses and print vendors who have experience in FM screening or in high-frequency halftoning (200 lpi and higher).

- **Proofing**—Accurate proofing is still problematic for FM-screened images, since existing proofing systems can't reproduce such tiny dot sizes or reflect the extra amount of dot gain. As FM screening gains acceptance, expect development of appropriate proofing methods.

Tuning in to FM

Although several issues in FM screening remain partially unresolved, there *are* many imaging applications that can achieve striking benefits from this technology. Use the following guidelines to determine whether exploring FM screening could be viable for your projects.

Direct-to-Plate or Direct-to-Press Applications

FM screening requires extra attention to environmental quality assurance issues to control dot gain. The use of platesetters or direct-to-press systems reduces the number of steps involved in generating printed pages and therefore helps to hold the dot size. FM screening and direct-to-plate/press are a natural match!

High-Bit Color

FM screening excels at reproducing subtle tonal transitions, especially in highlights and shadows. Drum scans and 48-bit image-editing programs such as Live Picture are also known for retaining the smoothest possible tonal transitions in an image during the correction process. To preserve shading and detail all the way from input to final output, consider using FM screening for high-bit color images.

Intricately Detailed Images

Extremely detailed images often don't reproduce well in print using digital halftoning. The tiny dot sizes possible with FM screening help preserve the most intricate level of detail, provided that the prepress and print vendors understand how to control the higher dot gain.

HiFi Color and Extra Color Plates

HiFi color, discussed in greater detail in Chapter 4, describes a varied set of prepress technologies designed to improve the color gamut of printing through the use of more than four color plates. As we've already explained, using more than four plates with digital halftoning increases the risk of plate misalignment and moiré. FM screening, which eliminates moiré, is a perfect match to HiFi color printing and to CMYK print applications that require additional plates for metallic or fluorescent inks or varnishes.

Vendors with Experience

Regardless of what type of images you plan to output using FM screening, there's no substitute for prepress and print vendors who have had some experience with the technology—and who understand the value of communicating regularly and clearly with one another. Three-way communication between prepress service provider, printer, and design team is always important, but it's especially critical when you're dealing with a newer technology that entails delicate quality assurance measures. For the sake of ensuring consistency in output methods, consider using a full-service print vendor who generates film or plates in-house.

In this chapter we've taken a closer look at screening technologies, which are both the heart and soul of print reproduction and the cause of many challenges to flawless output. Dot gain and moirés aren't the only pitfalls that plague printed images: color casts, color imbalances, tonal compression, improper sharpening, excess or inadequate resolution, poor trapping, banding, and lack of information about press setups can cause equally annoying bugaboos. Chapters 4 through 10 deal with the best techniques for avoiding these and other print reproduction errors.

Color Reproduction and Management

olor excites attention, creates a mood, and enhances the impact of any message that it accompanies. As the tools for scanning, manipulating, and printing color images become steadily more affordable and user-friendly at the desktop level, it's no wonder that the use of color in print communications continues to increase.

Although the *use* of color may be on the rise, the level of *satisfaction* with the printed results often lags woefully behind. One reason for all the frustration stems from the fact that many users don't take the trouble to educate themselves about the basics of color reproduction; they often have expectations that are too high or make mistakes that could easily be avoided. A second reason has to do with the fact that there are fundamental differences between the way the human eye perceives color, and the means by which scanners, monitors, analog and digital cameras, and printing inks reproduce it. Making yourself aware of these differences is a little like studying a map of land mines in a foreign battle zone: if you know where to step carefully, you can reach

39

your destination safely—and perhaps even win the war.

In this chapter, we provide a map of the land mines involved in color print reproduction and survey some of the most useful tools that have been developed for navigating the various "languages" of color. Our goal, of course, is to help you increase your own level of satisfaction with the final, printed versions of the images in your projects.

Color Spaces

Apples are red, the sky is blue, and grass is green. But there are many varieties of apples, the depth of blue in the sky changes according to the time of day, and grass may lean toward brown or yellow depending on the season, how dry the weather is, and the species of grass. Even in "analog" nature, there's tremendous variation among everyday colors that we take for granted. To complicate matters further, our snapshots rarely match our memories, and when we tell someone else about something spectacular we've seen, there's no guarantee that the picture he or she has in mind will match, even remotely, the colors we saw. How, then, can we communicate color precisely?

These examples show how complex the task of describing color in exact, universal terms can be. That's the goal to which color scientists have committed themselves. Without universal "languages" of color and without a way to define color in standardized, numerical terms, scanning, image editing, and digital output would be unthinkable.

Color spaces, also called *color models*, are the means by which science describes color in conceptual and quantifiable terms. With a basic grasp of the conceptual representation of color, you can understand the relationships between colors when working with tone curves or selecting colors by number using a color picker in an image-editing package (see Figure 4–1). If you wonder why there are so many different letters in the alphabet soup, it's because multiple color spaces have been developed to meet the needs of specific industries or groups in describing how light is transmitted, absorbed, or reflected by specific media.

> **"Without universal 'languages' of color, digital image editing and output would be unthinkable."**

Whatever its basis, every color space must satisfy three requirements. It must specify color in a standardized way that doesn't rely on the capabilities of any single transitory device. It must also delineate the *gamut*, or range, of the colors it describes (no set of colors is infinite). Finally, it must account for the way in which the perception, transmission, or reflection of light determines that gamut. There are many different color spaces, but they all belong to one of three types: perceptual, additive, and subtractive. Those of us involved in producing images for print media have to be most concerned with three color spaces: CIE, a perceptual color space; RGB, an additive color space; and CMYK, a subtractive color space. Figures C–4 and C–5 in the Color Gallery illustrate how color science represents these color spaces visually.

Perceptual Color Spaces

For designers, artists, and photographers, the ultimate reference for color is the human eye. Our eyes can perceive only a small fraction of existing electromagnetic wavelengths; but even

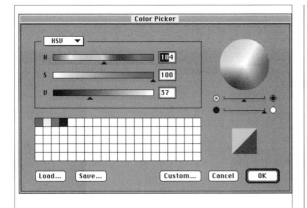

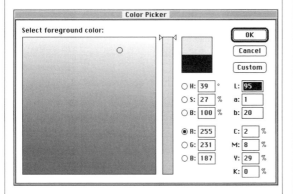

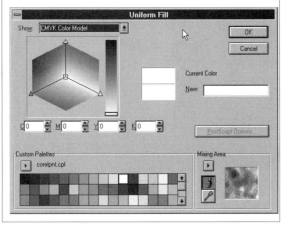

Figure 4–1

Top to bottom: *color pickers for the HSV (Hue, Saturation, Value) color space in Live Picture, the CIE LAB color space in Adobe Photoshop, and the CMYK color space in Corel PhotoPAINT!*

so, the visible spectrum comprises billions of colors—far more than any scanner, printer, or imagesetter can reproduce.

The perceptual color spaces used most widely today are variants of the one first developed in the 1920s by the CIE (Commission Internationale de l'Eclairage). The three–dimensional CIE color space (see Figure C–4 in the Color Gallery) describes any perceptible color in terms of values on a three-dimensional axis. One value describes *luminance* (the brightness component of a color, which has no color itself), while the other two relate to actual *chroma* or color values.

CIE color, like visual perception, is device independent. It also contains and is larger than both the RGB and CMYK gamuts, which is why color management software uses CIE color as the basis for translating colors safely between the more limited gamuts of input and output devices. Related perceptual color spaces with which imaging professionals are more familiar are the YCC color space used for Photo CD and the LAB color space used by Adobe Photoshop.

YCC and LAB Color

Photo CD workstations scan images as RGB data but then encode them for storage in a color space called *YCC*, which is a variant of the perceptual CIE color space. In YCC color, the Y channel value represents luminance, while the two C channel values represent the color ranges from magenta to green and from yellow to blue, respectively. When you download a Photo CD image to your computer by opening it in RGB or CMYK mode, the "color translation" entails further loss of the color data in the Photo CD image. One alternative to prematurely "fixing" the color range of a Photo CD image within a limited RGB or CMYK gamut as soon as you download it is to open it in Photoshop's CIE LAB color space. This strategy is especially useful when you need to begin working with a Photo CD image *before* you have all the necessary specifications about press setup and color separation. In the LAB color space, the L channel controls brightness and contrast like the Y channel in YCC, while the A and B channels control the same color ranges as the CC channels in YCC. As you'll see in Chapter 10, it's feasible to make tonal adjustments and apply sharpening to a Photo CD image while it's still in LAB mode.

The quality of the software you use to open a Photo CD image can also determine how well the color space translation optimizes the data in the image. Sophisticated utilities, such as CD/Q from Human Software and PhotoImpress from Display Technologies, for example, perform an entire set of prepress enhancements to Photo CD images on the fly as they are opened in CMYK mode.

Note: *Artists and designers traditionally have used the HLS (hue, lightness, saturation) and HSB (hue, saturation, brightness) or HSV (V for variance) color spaces for specifying color. These color spaces are intuitive (based on a rainbow color scheme) and are represented in most digital color pickers. Hue is measured in terms of degrees that represent a hue's position on a circular color wheel.*

Additive Color Spaces

The RGB color space is the natural color "language" of electronic input devices such as computer monitors, scanners, and digital cameras, which reproduce color by transmitting or absorbing light rather than by reflecting it. The color you see on computer monitors, for example, comes about when electron beams strike red, green, and blue phosphors coating the screen, causing those phosphors to emit light in varying combinations—up to 16.7 million possible colors if you use a 24-bit color display adapter (important for color publishing work).

> **❝***The RGB color space is the natural color 'language' of electronic input devices such as monitors, scanners, and digital cameras.***❞**

We call the RGB model an *additive* color space because colors are generated by adding colored light to colored light. Secondary colors are therefore always brighter than the red, green, and/or blue primaries that combine to create them. Adding maximum intensities of red, green, and blue produces white in the RGB color space (see Figure C–5 in the Color Gallery). Combining equal values of red, green, and blue produces neutral shades of gray, with low values producing darker grays and high values producing lighter ones.

Sixteen million colors may seem like an infinite number, but as a comparison of Figures C–4 and C–5 in the Color Gallery reveals, RGB color has a much narrower gamut than the visible spectrum. Even so, the color gamut that monitors can display is sufficient for photorealistic editing. Keep in mind, though, that the RGB color space is *device dependent*; the colors generated from any individual RGB device may differ from those that another RGB device can reproduce.

Subtractive Color Spaces

If you subtract one of the primary RGB colors from white light, you obtain colors complementary to red, green, and blue. Green and blue with red subtracted produce cyan; red and blue with green subtracted produce magenta; and red and green with blue subtracted yield yellow. Surprise! You have CMY, three of the four components of the CMYK color space that is the basis for color mixing in the printing industry.

In a *subtractive* color space like CMYK, mixing two or more primaries generates additional colors by transmitting some light waves and absorbing others. Cyan ink, for example, absorbs red light and transmits green and blue; magenta ink absorbs green light and transmits red and blue; and yellow ink absorbs blue light and transmits red and green. Whereas in the additive RGB model light is added to light, producing brighter colors, in the subtractive CMYK model light is subtracted, producing darker colors. Add to that the opaque nature of paper, which reflects light rather than transmitting it, and you can better understand why the colors in an image that looks brilliant on your monitor appear darker and duller when they are printed. If your image-editing package or color management software allows it, preview images in CMYK as you work in RGB mode to accurately forecast and correct for the CMYK color gamut.

Note: The medium of reproduction has more to do with perceived brightness than does the color space itself. Photographic transparencies and photographic prints, for example, both use CMY dyes, but the transparencies have a broader dynamic range because light passes through the transparent dyes and then directly to the eyes of the viewer. In a print, light first passes through the dyes, and then is reflected off the paper, reducing the light's intensity.

The RGB and CMY color spaces are complementary to one another, at least in theory. Mixing equal amounts of cyan, magenta, and yellow should produce neutral grays, and mixing maximum amounts should produce black (the complement of white in the RGB color space). They do so on the monitor, but on press, reality falls short of the ideal. Mixing maximum amounts of CMY inks produces not black but muddy brown. The reason for this phenomenon is that there are inherent impurities in commercial-quality pigments and inks. Cyan inks are usually a little too blue, while magenta and yellow inks are usually a little too red. Due to these imbalances, an RGB grayscale prints with a reddish or purplish cast when converted to straight CMY.

That's where black comes to the rescue. Black is the *key color* (K) that printers add to cyan, magenta, and yellow to produce deeper, richer blacks and shadow tones with crisper definition. Of course, the addition of a fourth color skews the RGB-to-CMYK conversion equation, making it more complex to juggle color correspondences between RGB and CMYK. There's no simple one-to-one correspondence anyway; the CIE color representation in Figure C–4 shows that although the RGB and CMYK color gamuts overlap, they don't match exactly. Printers' inks can't reproduce intense blues and greens, even though monitors can. Many eye-pleasing colors on your monitor can't be reproduced using printers' inks. To prove this for yourself, use your image-editing or color management software to preview an RGB image in CMYK, or try activating Photoshop's Gamut Warning command on a particularly brilliant RGB image. You'll quickly find out just how much of it is unprintable without modifying color and tonal range!

When you convert an image from RGB to CMYK, the amount of black you want (and the tonal ranges in which you want it to appear) get figured into a complex algorithm that determines just how RGB values shift in CMY terms. Separation parameters known as *GCR* (for *gray component replacement*) and *UCR* (for *under color removal*) correct for the addition of black *and* for the CMY pigment impurities during the conversion process; we'll discuss them in Chapter 6. The conversion process also automatically corrects for the fact that (again due to ink impurities) the cyan plate must print heavier than the magenta and yellow plates in order to produce a neutral gray. For this reason, whenever you convert a digital RGB image to the CMYK mode, a deliberate imbalance toward cyan occurs. The exact amount of this imbalance depends on your software setup for color separations (see Chapter 6); but, in general, you can expect a cyan value that's 2 or 3 percentage points darker than magenta and yellow in the lightest grays, increasing to 12 to 15 percent darker in the midtones (50 percent gray), and decreasing again to 7 to 10 percent darker in the shadows (see Figure 4–2). A final complication to the CMYK color space is that it's device dependent, thanks to the equipment on which it's based. Just as every monitor and scanner reproduces RGB color a little differently, so every type of color printer, proofing system, and press setup reproduces a slightly different segment of the overall CMYK gamut. This inherent device dependency among RGB and CMYK devices is one reason why calibration and color management are so important for print publications professionals working with color images.

Color Depth

The *color depth* or *bit depth* of an image determines the image's file size, its dynamic range from dark to light, and the maximum number of colors that will reproduce in print.

- *Bitmap* or *line art* (1-bit) images consist of black and white pixels only. Each pixel contains only one bit of information, so file sizes are compact. For best output results, the resolution of line art should be equal to the resolution of the final output device or 1,200 ppi, whichever is lower (see Chapter 10).

- *Grayscale* images (8-bit) represent all the tones and colors in the original using up to 256 shades of gray. Each pixel contains eight bits of information, so files are eight times as large as for comparably sized originals scanned in line art mode.

- *Indexed color* images (also 8-bit) use a limited palette of 256 colors. File size is approximately the same as for grayscale images. Indexed color has little support in printing

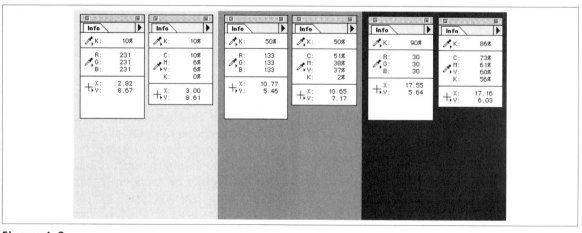

Figure 4–2

This gray ramp, produced using equal amounts of red, green, and blue in the RGB color space, shows an imbalance toward heavier cyan values when converted to the CMYK color space. This imbalance occurs because printers' inks are inherently impure and cyan needs to print darker than magenta and yellow in order to produce a neutral gray.

unless you're planning spot color separations; you usually need to convert a 256-color image to the RGB or CMYK mode in order to edit or output it. It's useful for creating special color-reduction effects.

- *RGB color* (24-bit) images reproduce up to 16 million colors in three 8-bit channels (256 colors per channel). File sizes for an RGB image are 24 times as large as a comparable bitmap and 3 times as large as a grayscale.

- *CMYK color* (32-bit) images are preseparated for color print output. Bit depth is the same as for RGB images (8 bits, or 256 colors per channel), but file sizes are one-third larger because they contain an extra channel.

- *High-bit color* images have exceptionally broad dynamic ranges because they're produced by scanners and digital cameras that record color at 10 to 16 bits per channel—1,024 to 65,536 colors per channel, compared with 256 in standard RGB and CMYK images. Files are 36 to 48 times as large as a comparable bitmap and 4.5 to 6 times as large as a grayscale of the same size; but when handled correctly, they can deliver excellent detail in print, especially when output using FM screening, HiFi color separations, or both. Not all image-editing packages support editing in high-bit color.

Color Printing Devices

The quantity of the anticipated print run, the project budget, the intended audience, and the quality of proofing you require are the factors that determine how you'll print a document, both for the final job and at intermediate proofing stages. For long print runs, the most economical final printing methods to use are four-color offset, sheetfed, or newspaper presses (or sometimes flexo or gravure presses). But for short-run documents, such as limited-distribution corporate reports, in-house newsletters, real estate flyers, and the like, small-format color printers are often economical enough to serve as the final output device. Graphic arts professionals also use such printers as preliminary proofing devices for higher-end documents for which a long print run is projected. See the sidebar "Proofing for Print Reproduction Pitfalls" for more information about the relative advantages and disadvantages of color proofing methods.

> **❝ Print run, budget, intended audience, and quality of proofing determine how you'll print a document. ❞**

The quality of output from color printing devices varies greatly. Here are the major types of devices and their recommended uses in the prepress cycle:

- *Phase-change inkjet printers* use solid CMY or CMYK inks, which melt into a small reservoir and then spray onto the paper or substrate in extremely fine drops to simulate continuous tone. These printers can output to many types and sizes of paper or other media, which makes them convenient to use. The output from low- to medium-resolution inkjet printers has a more or less grainy look, but higher-end (and higher-resolution) inkjet devices, such as the Iris Realist line of printers (Figure 4–3), simulate continuous-tone color well. Even midrange devices like the Epson Stylus Pro series are improving the quality and fidelity of inkjet color. Use low-end

Figure 4–3

courtesy Iris Corp.

The Realist 5015 and 5030 inkjet printers from Iris output at an effective resolution of 1,800 dpi and feature imaging areas of 14 x 21 inches and 21 x 28 inches, respectively.

Figure 4–4

courtesy Tektronix

The Tektronix Phaser 540 Plus, a 600 x 300 dpi color laser printer, uses variably sized toner spots to divert attention from halftone patterning.

inkjet output for draft- or *comp*-quality proofing only, to ensure that all elements are in place and that the overall color balance is correct. For jobs where color quality isn't critical, press shops have been known to accept mirrange or high-end inkjet output as final proofs for press matching.

- *Thermal-wax transfer printers* use a roll of colored wax that contains pigments for the separate CMY or CMYK colors. The output medium (paper or transparency) passes under the printhead once for each color, and tiny areas of color on the wax roll are melted onto it. Use thermal-wax transfer printers for comp-quality proofs only.

- *Color laser printers*, like their monochrome siblings, use fine plastic toners that are electrostatically attracted to a drum, transferred to the page, and then fixed to the page as the paper passes through a pair of fusing rollers. Most color lasers use halftone patterning, which allows you to preview potential moiré problems (provided the printer resolution and requested screen frequency approximate those of the final output

device) and trapping errors (see Figure 4–4). Some newer-model color lasers use a fine diffusion dither pattern instead of digital halftoning; for these, the foregoing statement doesn't apply. You can use a wide variety of papers with color lasers, and newer laser devices provide excellent color registration. On the downside, color consistency is difficult to achieve with laser printers due to variations in toner chromaticities and the way in which toner settles in the cartridge over a period of time.

- *Dye sublimation printers* (see Figure 4–5) produce photorealistic, continuous-tone color by subtly varying the temperatures in the heating elements that melt the CMYK dyes. Hotter temperatures cause more dye to be vaporized and transferred to the paper, resulting in darker or more intense colors. Although dye sublimation printers can't simulate dot gain or moiré problems, a few higher-end dye sublimation printers can reproduce potential trapping errors. Some print shops are willing to accept dye sublimation output for noncritical color matching on press.

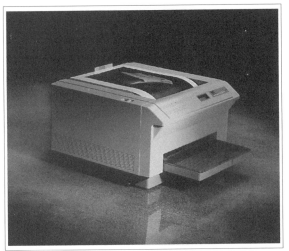

Figure 4–5

courtesy 3M Corp.

The 3M Rainbow proofer, a 300 dpi dye sublimation printer, can simulate color from a variety of press setups, including sheet-fed, web offset, and newsprint.

Caution: *Don't consider the color from color printers as reliable indications of what to expect on press. Colors vary from one manufacturer's implementation to another or in the same piece of equipment over time, and the substrates used in small-format devices differ from printers' inks.*

Separated Color

When large print quantities indicate the use of an offset or other type of press as the final printing device, color separations are in order before you're ready to print. Depending on your budget, press setup, and the type of documents you produce, you can output color separations to paper, film, or plates. Separated color usually takes one of three forms: duotones, process-color separations, and HiFi color. The type and number of separations planned for an image determines how many channels the digital version contains. We'll include more information about channels in Chapter 5.

Spot Color and Duotones

When the aim is to apply only one to three pure or custom ink colors to an image on press, it's economical to create spot color separations using PANTONE inks or nonstandard process inks. The best known way to create spot color separations digitally is through Photoshop's patented Duotone feature, which can combine two, three, or four spot colors in an image. *Duotones* (combinations of two colors) usually include black plus one other color; the relative amounts of each color can be varied at any point along the tonal range. Third-party plug-ins such as PlateMaker from IN Software and PhotoSpot from Second Glance Software offer other alternatives for generating spot color separations. Refer to Chapter 6 for information on creating and color separating duotones and other forms of spot-color separations.

Process Color

When you print a document using the familiar four-color (CMYK) process inks, you need to generate process-color separations for the images. Creating color separations requires mastery of what often seems to be a tremendous amount of complex information, so many imaging end users prefer to let a service bureau or color prepress house do the dirty work. Our position in this book is that the process of process color isn't as impossible as you might think. If you take the trouble to find out a few details about press setup and communicate closely with prepress and print vendors, you can climb the hurdles of file formats, total ink limits, black ink limits, UCR, GCR, UCA, and the rest of the CMYK alphabet soup. Chapter 6 will guide you step by step through the color separation maze.

Tip: *Unless you know all press setup details well in advance, edit an image in RGB mode and convert to CMYK for final tonal and color correction only as the time for final output nears. Converting to CMYK using the wrong information can skew colors incorrectly.*

HiFi Color

Professionals in advertising and packaging, whose profitability depends heavily on the impact of color messages, have long been disgruntled about the narrow gamut of colors that CMYK inks can reproduce. The four-color process can generate decent reds, but vivid blues, greens, pinks, violets, browns, and many other photographic colors are impossible to achieve, and saturation is often disappointing even in colors that reproduce well.

Out of this frustration, an evolving movement known as *HiFi color* has been born. HiFi color solutions take many different forms depending on the manufacturer, but common to all implementations are strategies to extend the gamut of color printing through the use of more than four color separations. LinoType-Hell's HiFi Color 3000 system, for example, uses seven colors (CMYK plus RGB) to produce more vibrant reds, greens, and blues. PANTONE's Hexachrome uses CMYK plus custom-formulated orange and green colorants, while DuPont's HyperColor system uses a second set of CMY separations for five-, six-, or seven-color printing, depending on image content.

Products like these are generally found only in color prepress houses and service bureaus. For do-it-yourselfers who prefer to separate their own files, stand-alone applications and Photoshop plug-ins at various price ranges are available. LinoType-Hell's EderMCS, for example, allows end users who have already saved files in CMYK mode to convert them into HiFi color separations containing five, six, or seven

plates. TransCal's HiFi ColorSeps plug-in creates extra separations that can be HiFi color oriented or intended for metallic, varnish, or other custom colors. It exports files to the DCS EPS format. Lowly Apprentice Productions' PlateMaker (Figure 4–6) works within Photoshop to generate up to 24 separations for HiFi color or custom colors and can also create up to 256 spot color separations in Indexed Color mode for screen printing applications.

Gaps still remain to be filled in the areas of scanner profiles, color management, and reliable proofing for HiFi color separations, but the technology is rapidly gaining acceptance for high-end color printing. HiFi color works well with FM screening (which eliminates the concern over moirés when additional plates must be printed) and with images scanned or photographed in high-bit color.

Note: *The use of additional color plates doesn't mean that HiFi color separations require more ink on press. Many HiFi color solutions use less total ink than conventional CMYK separations do. HiFi separations achieve their characteristically brilliant colors by virtue of the more-intense pigments of the extra inks used.*

The Color Management Quest

Once upon a time, before the advent of "open" desktop publishing systems, you could count on somebody else's expertise to scan, correct, and output the images in your documents. Color consistency from input to print was virtually assured, because all the operations were performed on big-budget, proprietary systems from a single vendor. The process worked well, but it was expensive, and end users had little control.

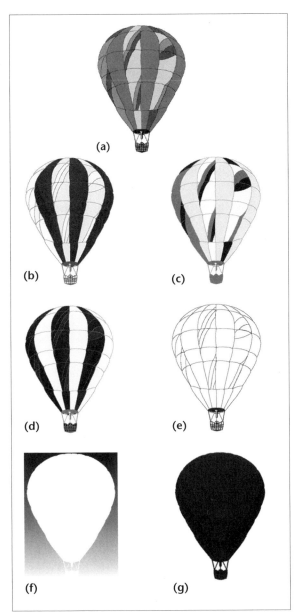

Figure 4–6

Lowly Apprentice Productions' PlateMaker can create up to 24 process color separations or up to 256 spot color separations from within Photoshop. Files are saved in EPS DCS 2.0 format. The example shows a CMYK original (a, reproduced here in grayscale) and a six-plate separation (b–g) that uses extra plates for a PANTONE spot color plus a varnish.

Nowadays, end users have affordable color and plenty of control—and the chaos and responsibility that come with it. Print communications professionals routinely combine scanners, monitors, software, computers, printers, proofing systems, imagesetters, and platesetters from different manufacturers. Many collaborators in a prepress project don't even work on the same computer platform. Unfortunately, each type of input or output device, each manufacturer's model of a given device, and even each individual unit within a product line has a unique gamut and reproduces color differently. Yet, in spite of this absence of standardization, you're often expected to produce color that's beyond eye-pleasing—color that exactly *matches* an undigitized original or what you see on your monitor. To a certain extent, this goal is unattainable because of the device-dependent nature of the RGB and CMYK color spaces. There's also the larger question of whether you should slavishly match an original, or whether you should instead enhance color, tone, and sharpness to more fully realize the *intent* of the original. But when matching needs to be as close and consistent as technologically possible, good *color management* practices can help.

Just what constitutes good color management for your applications depends on your budget, the kinds of documents you typically produce, your press setup requirements, and the number of colleagues or vendors (and computer systems) involved in your projects. The more varied your projects and the more critical the color in your documents, the more sophisticated your color management setup should be. There are three levels of sophistication among color management products and practices. Here they are, from the simplest to the most complex:

■ *Calibration* is the process of regularly adjusting each input and output device in your system so that it reproduces color according to the manufacturer's specifications, and it is

Proofing for Print Reproduction Pitfalls

The goal of color proofing is to forecast and correct for potential problems that might occur on press. Proofing should occur several times during the production cycle. Initially, it may take place during the design development phase, when approval of the composition is the highest priority. Later on, a color proof gives evidence of overall color balance. At the time of output, a final *contract proof* should be generated—one that accurately reflects color, simulates dot gain, reproduces registration and moiré problems, and reveals potential trapping and banding errors.

In practice, the publication's budget, paper stock, and press setup determine what constitutes a contract-quality proof acceptable to the print vendor. Let's first survey the types of errors that an ideal color proof should detect and then evaluate the best match between proofing technologies and publication types.

Print Reproduction Pitfalls

Digital images are especially prone to the following common problems that degrade the quality of a print job. Chapters 6 through 8 describe suggestions for eliminating these problems during the image enhancement and color separation process.

- **Color casts**—Undesirable color shifts toward a specific hue can appear in print, even when they're not easily detectable on a computer monitor. Common causes include poor photographic lighting, an uncalibrated system, or failure to detect and correct for the cast.

- **Dot gain**—Halftone dots can spread during electronic output or on press (FM-screened dots are even more subject to this malady; see Chapter 3). Larger halftone dots result in a darkening of the colors in the printed version of an image, especially in the midtones and shadow areas.

- **Misregistration (trapping and moiré)**—Mislignment of color plates on press—sometimes by as little as two-thousandths of an inch—can cause noticeable flaws in a printed image. One common type of registration flaw is the moiré patterning with which you're already familiar from Chapter 3. Another type of problem occurs when large areas of solid color abut another color in an image, causing an unsightly ghosting effect. Creating adequate trapping for these areas of adjacent colors—a subject we take up in Chapter 9—prevents this kind of error.

Note: Trapping isn't usually a problem for continuous-tone color unless an image contains areas of solid color, as with posterized images or hand-drawn illustrations that have been digitized.

- **Banding**—When an image includes a gradient that contains too few steps for the distance covered, a stair-stepping or banding effect becomes visible. Banding is a headache for vector drawings but rarely a problem for continuous-tone images, unless the color range of the gradient is narrow or the output device uses a screen frequency that's too high for the device's resolution.

Types of Proofing

Not every kind of color proof can reflect the types of flaws likely to show up on press. There are three basic categories of proofs, each suitable for different uses:

- *Digital proofs* are color proofs from inkjet, thermal-wax transfer, color laser, dye sublimation, or direct digital printers. No film separations are involved, so these proofs can't represent high-frequency screening, dot gain, or moiré patterning accurately. Faithful color reproduction *is* possible with high-resolution inkjet and continuous-tone dye sublimation printers, however, and a few advanced dye sublimation devices can also reveal trapping errors. Some press shops accept dye sublimation and high-end inkjet output as contract proofs for jobs that aren't color critical, such as publications printed on absorbent papers at line screens below 133 lpi.

- *Film-based proofs* are generated from the actual film separations that will be used to make plates. These include *laminate proofs*, which are created by laminating the film separations onto a single sheet (not paper) and *overlay proofs*, which consist of layers of acetate (one for each film separation) overlaid atop one another to show the composite image. Both laminate and overlay proofs are acceptable as contract-quality proofs. Laminate proofing systems are especially well regarded for their color quality and their ability to reflect dot gain, registration, and banding with relative accuracy. Fuji Matchprint and 3M Matchprint are examples of popular laminate proofing systems.

- *Press proofs* use the actual printing press, inks, and paper stocks planned for the final print run. This makes them extremely accurate for predicting possible problems, but also very expensive.

Note: *Expect new types of proofing systems that can accurately predict potential problems in HiFi color and FM-screened images.*

---

the foundation of all color management. It's everyone's responsibility.

- *Color management system (CMS) software* is useful for anyone who regularly obtains images from more than one input source or outputs to more than one type of device. Most CMS products let you store information about the color characteristics of many devices and use that information to translate image colors from the color space of any saved device to the color space of any other. But in order for a CMS product to work well, it should support all the devices and computer platforms involved in the production cycle for a project. See the "CMS Solutions" section later in this chapter for guidelines.

- *Hardware calibration or color measurement devices* are essential for high-end color print projects, where exact color matching is required and where manual or software-only calibration methods may be too subjective for hairbreadth technical accuracy. They're also a handy adjunct to the many CMS products that allow you to generate custom device color characterizations to supplement the provided presets.

The Calibration Process

The color reproduction characteristics of every monitor, color printer, imagesetter, and other input or output device tend to vary over time.

It's important to adjust, or *calibrate*, the performance of each device regularly in order to ensure that it conforms to the manufacturer's standards. Without frequent calibration of the input and output components in your system, even the best CMS software package can't do the job it was meant to do. Monitors are the least stable device in any system, so if you do nothing else, make certain that your monitor gets calibrated at least once a month (once a day if you work with high volumes of images).

The ideal calibration process involves several steps. Begin by standardizing your *color environment*—the lighting and colors in the area where you work. Other steps include calibrating your scanner, monitor, and output devices individually; printing a color proof; and adjusting devices to compensate for noted color inconsistencies.

Standardizing the Color Environment

Many factors, from subjective emotions to external lighting conditions, influence how the human eye perceives color. We can't account for emotions, of course, but it *is* possible to control many of the objective factors in the environment where you work. Observe these guidelines to ensure that your environment is as free from distracting variables as possible:

- Scan and view images in an area free from glare, where lighting doesn't change much over the course of the day (and night, if you're a workaholic). If this isn't possible, at least try to perform the critical color-related imaging tasks at the same time each day. Use blinds in rooms that have many windows, and consistent, neutral lighting in rooms that have none.

- Make sure that the wall coloring in your work area is neutral, subdued, and uniform.

- Bright colors surrounding images can distort your perception of the image colors, so set the background color of your monitor to a neutral gray. Dispense with digital wallpaper for the sake of perceiving the colors of images more accurately.

Calibrating Monitors

Having established a consistent color environment, the next step is to calibrate the monitor on which you view scanned images. An uncalibrated monitor can introduce apparent color casts into images, which may not faithfully represent the contents of the digital files. For best results, calibrate a monitor only after it has been running for at least a half hour to ensure that its colors have stabilized.

There are three basic types of tools for calibrating monitors: software utilities that ship with image-editing packages, hardware-based calibrators, and the monitor profiles that are part of color management systems. Together, the volume of scanning work that you process and the image-editing package you use will dictate which of the three approaches best serves your needs.

Caution: *Avoid using more than one type of monitor calibration tool simultaneously. Each utility or device can skew the results of the others. If you work with multiple image-editing packages, use a third-party color management system or hardware calibration device.*

Image-editing calibration utilities Most image-editing packages include a software utility for calibrating monitor display. Some utilities offer only basic options, such as adjusting the representation of grays and colors to eliminate color casts. Others can even compensate for the chromaticity values of the red, green, and blue phosphors produced by a specific brand of monitor. The Gamma utility (see Figure 4–7), developed by Knoll Software and shipped with Adobe Photoshop, is an

example of such a software utility. The Gamma utility allows you to adjust many monitor display parameters, including

■ The neutral, linear representation of gray shades

■ The monitor's white and black points (the brightest and darkest shades that the monitor's phosphors can display)

■ The *gamma curve* of the monitor, which adjusts a monitor's ability to distribute tones evenly between its white and black points

■ Color balance, through direct manipulation of red, green, and blue phosphor emissions

The Gamma utility also allows you to save and load multiple calibration settings for various purposes, such as variable lighting conditions or matching a monitor's display characteristics to paper stocks for separate projects.

Hardware calibration devices   Service bureaus, ad agencies, and other environments with high-volume scanning needs may find a hardware calibration device more convenient to use than a software utility. Hardware calibration devices—typically consisting of a suction-cup sensor that attaches to the monitor, plus accompanying calibration software like the example shown in Figure 4–8—stabilize viewing conditions on a monitor for display consistency. Graphic arts professionals traditionally measure these conditions in terms of Kelvin temperature. The standard for viewing most color print work is 5,000 degrees Kelvin, equivalent to the color of white seen under bright sunlight at noon. But most monitors have a white color temperature between 6,300 and 9,300 degrees Kelvin and don't produce good-quality output at 5,000 degrees. Hardware calibration devices adjust the monitor's white point to the desired Kelvin temperature for that unit, automatically adjusting all the other colors that the monitor can display. Such devices also allow you to calibrate the monitor's brightness curve and color balance.

Tip: Even with a device-calibrated monitor, it's still essential to generate proofs and view them in the lighting conditions under which your audience will view the final document.

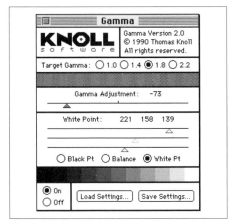

Figure 4–7

Knoll Software's Gamma utility provided with Photoshop (here in its Macintosh version)

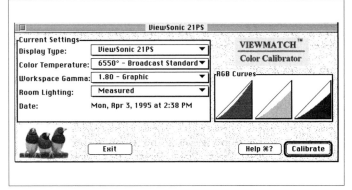

Figure 4–8

The ViewMatch Color Calibrator, developed jointly by ViewSonic and Sequel Imaging, intelligently measures ambient lighting and calibrates monitor colors and grays, as well as white and black points. It saves monitor data as a custom color profile in an ICC-compatible format.

Hardware calibration devices work well in concert with color management systems because they allow you to save information about a monitor's characteristics to disk. The trend these days is to specify this information in a format that both system-level and third-party CMS software can read.

Color management profiles Many color management software packages (see "CMS Solutions" later in this chapter) include a module for comparing your monitor's display characteristics with the standards set by the manufacturer. If your brand of monitor doesn't appear in the CMS's library of preset profiles, some CMSs may be able to generate a custom profile based on information recorded by a compatible hardware calibrator or that you input manually.

Matching Display Color to Input and Output

Adjusting a monitor is only part of the calibration equation. What you see on your screen should be faithful to the way the input device represents colors, if at least both the source image and the input device are high quality. (Originals and scanners that are less than ideal may require that you be faithful to an image's intent, not to its literal input characteristics.). It should also match the colors in any proofing device you may use, as well as the colors of the final output. Even if you don't use a CMS, you can calibrate scanners and printers for internal consistency and coordinate the color characteristics of a single production system manually.

The key to manual system calibration is having some kind of *reference image* that you can pass through the system from input to output. The reference image can be an actual reflective or transparent original (depending on the kind of scanner you're using), or it can be a standard grayscale or color *target* supplied with your scanner. The latter is preferable, since

> **❝***The standard for viewing most color print work is 5,000 degrees Kelvin, equivalent to the color of white seen under bright sunlight at noon.***❞**

your sample image may represent less than the full range of colors and/or tones that industry-standard targets contain. Calibrate your system by following these steps:

1. Calibrate your monitor using one of the methods described in this chapter.
2. Calibrate your scanner internally, if necessary. High-end drum, flatbed, and film/transparency scanners calibrate themselves automatically each time you turn them on. Most other scanners require manual calibration approximately once a month to compensate for color shifts that occur over time. Many midrange flatbed scanner manufacturers supply a grayscale or color target with their equipment and include special calibration software.

Tip: Hook up your scanner to a line conditioner to keep fluctuations in electrical current from influencing CCD readings.

3. Scan the reference image or industry-standard target into the calibrated scanner.
4. Read the 50 percent patch in both grayscale and RGB to ensure that the scanner's gamma is set properly.
5. Compare the image on your monitor with the undigitized original and make

further adjustments to the display as necessary.

6. Make sure that your color printer (or color proofing device at an off-site service provider, the film recorder, or other service vendor) is internally calibrated for consistency according to the manufacturer's recommended method.

7. Using your image-editing software, make adjustments for dot gain, CMYK ink balance, paper stock, and other factors that affect color printing output to your chosen device. This may be the most important step in the procedure! Chapter 6 covers guidelines for these.

8. Output the image to the color proofing device or other medium of your choice.

9. Compare the output results with both the monitor display and the undigitized original. Make further adjustments to input and display equipment, if required.

As you can imagine, manual calibration is a trial-and-error process that may require several iterations to produce consistent results. The process becomes even more complicated if a project uses a variety of input and output devices at multiple locations. Juggling the color diplomacy of so many different standards is a task for color management system (CMS) software.

Tip: Scan an 18 percent gray card or graduated grayscale with a color original and use the scanned image as a calibration target. If the scanned grays have a color cast, tweak the target to calibrate your monitor and scanner.

CMS Principles

Calibrating all the devices in your system manually is a time-consuming and somewhat subjective process. It also doesn't go far enough if you regularly work with different designers,

color prepress houses, service bureaus, and vendors, since there are no guarantees that the color in your calibrated system will be consistent with the color in the system of the next party who exchanges files with you.

Color management systems create order out of this confusion by establishing a set of objective rules for communicating color between devices. These rules enable you to match the color in your system with the input or output devices on other systems remote from your location. In order to make the communication "language" universal, a CMS must account for three types of variables, each of which affects color representation at a different level:

- **Gamut**—Each *type* of device has a color gamut that's much more limited than the visual spectrum encompassed by CIE color. Scanners, monitors, Photo CD images, digital cameras, film recorders, and television sets represent color in RGB terms, while color printers, proofing devices, and presses use CMYK. A CMS navigates between RGB and CMYK devices using the broader CIE gamut, which contains both RGB and CMYK.

- **Profile**—Two flatbed scanners by different manufacturers rarely reproduce colors in the same way. One scanner may shift hues toward red, while another emphasizes greens. To account for differences in color representation at the brand name level, a CMS provides preset *profiles* that describe a particular product's color characteristics. Some CMSs also let you generate custom profiles for equipment brands for which no profiles exist. Most CMS products now support the industry-standard ICC (International Color Consortium) profile format, which defines what color characteristics a profile should describe.

- **Calibration**—Each unit of a given model may deviate slightly from the color representation standard specified by the manufacturer. A CMS typically includes calibration options so that you can measure and record any differences between the profile established for your equipment brand and the unique reproduction characteristics of your unit. The CMS can then compensate for these differences when translating color between devices.

A CMS's ability to describe *and record* the color characteristics of any input, display, or output device in the workflow (whether or not it is attached to your system) makes color consistency possible. Once this information exists digitally, the CMS can retrieve it and use it to negotiate color translations between separate devices in the production chain.

Managing Color—The Process

To use a color management system effectively, you need to follow a defined sequence of steps, which varies depending on the capabilities of a particular package. An ideal CMS procedure would follow this pattern:

1. *Characterize the color performance of the monitor.* Your monitor display mediates between input and output, so record its color characteristics first. Some color management systems provide a full complement of built-in presets from various monitor manufacturers, while others allow you to create a custom monitor profile, either by entering information manually or by using a hardware calibration device.

2. *Calibrate the monitor.* Its white point and other display characteristics should match the ideal parameters set forth in the color profile. Many CMS packages customize your monitor's profile to compensate for variances from the brand-name profile.

3. *Characterize the scanner or other input device.* If the CMS provides an industry-standard IT8 target like the ones pictured in the Color Gallery of *Scanning the Professional Way*, scan it. (If you're using a digital camera, capture an image of the target under controlled lighting conditions.) Open the resulting digital file and let the CMS compare the ideal color and gray tones of the target with the ones your input device generated. The CMS records variance information as a digital profile of the input device's color characteristics for future use.

4. *Use the CMS to transform the target scan to the color space of your monitor.* The CMS now converts the digitized target from the color space of the input device to the monitor's color space, using the color profiles it established for both devices. Most third-party color management systems perform this operation in Adobe Photoshop.

Note: *Color management packages compensate for a scanner's color characteristics only after an image is already scanned. They don't transform color on the fly.*

Caution: *Every CMS transform causes an image to lose data that can't be recovered. Keep the number of transforms in your workflow to a minimum to avoid unnecessary degradation.*

5. *Characterize your color proofer or other output device.* Select or define a profile for the color printer, press conditions, Photo CD, or other output device supported by the CMS.

6. *Output the target image to your chosen output device.* The CMS uses the profiles for monitor and printer (or scanner and printer) to convert image color during

this process. This can occur within an image-editing or page composition program. Some color management systems allow you to view a *soft proof* (an onscreen CMYK representation) of the image before printing.

CMS Solutions

Ideally, color management should take place at the operating system level. A computer's system software should support a single, standardized format for describing device-color characteristics. Additionally, all imaging and page layout applications on that platform should include calls to the CMS so that color transformation takes place automatically when you open an image or convert it from RGB to CMYK. Let's take that a step further: CMSs on all platforms should support the *same* standard for writing device-color profile information so that the colors in images transferred between platforms can remain predictable throughout the production cycle.

Although that ideal hasn't been realized, the industry is taking steps in that direction. Until recently, many stand-alone CMS products vied with one another for market share while each supported only a single platform, a limited number of software applications, and a proprietary type of device profile. Because of the lack of standards, device manufacturers were reluctant to write profiles, without which a CMS is useless. Imaging users who could potentially benefit from a CMS also showed little interest. Now, however, Apple's ColorSync 2.0 and color-matching routines built into Windows 95 hold the promise of more transparent future color management procedures (see the sidebar "Color Management at the Operating System Level").

Meanwhile, third-party stand-alone CMS products continue to flourish. No existing CMS is perfect, but several CMS packages have distinguished themselves for features such as

cross-platform compatibility, support for the ICC profile format, an extensive collection of device profiles, or flexible options for creating additional custom profiles. Let's take a brief look at some major players.

> **❝**CMSs should support the same standard for device profile information so that colors in images transferred between platforms can remain predictable throughout the production cycle.**❞**

Agfa FotoTune

Version 2 of Agfa's FotoTune is an exceptionally well thought out CMS that runs on both the Macintosh and Windows platforms. FotoTune ships with three industry-standard IT8 targets, two transmissive and one reflective. It also includes a veritable host of preset color profiles (which it calls *ColorTags*) for monitors, color printers, film recorders, color spaces, and even standard offset press setups. If these aren't enough for your needs, you can use the targets and the supplied color characterization utilities to create custom profiles for your devices.

Note: *FotoTune offers limited monitor characterization tools, relying on Photoshop's Gamma utility. But if you have a hardware calibration device that can create an ICC-compatible profile, FotoTune can read and use it.*

Ideally, a color management system should support color conversions and separations, not only to color proofing printers, but also to high-end press proofs and offset press scenarios that take press, paper, and ink considerations into account. In this respect, FotoTune follows through more thoroughly than many CMS products. It supplies four standard SWOP profiles, as well as four Euro-Ink profiles (for European end users) and multiple ColorTags for digital proofing devices. As Figure 4–9 shows, you can customize any of the offset press profiles, even to the extent of altering settings for color gamut, separation curves, total ink and black ink limits, and dot gain. And you can

optionally save any monitor, scanner, or printing profile in the ICC format supported by Apple ColorSync 2 and Windows 95.

For image color transformations, FotoTune supplies a plug-in for Adobe Photoshop and an XTension for QuarkXPress. You can correct a scan for monitor display, edit the image in Photoshop, and then generate CMYK separations using an output profile (which FotoTune optionally can save as a custom Photoshop separation table). If you plan to place a scanned image directly into a layout, you can

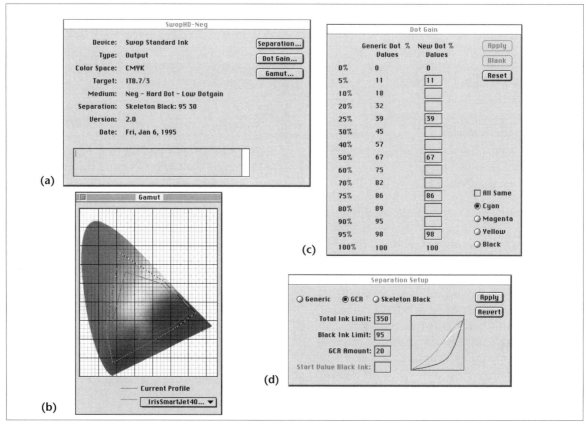

Figure 4–9

*FotoTune lets you customize any standard offset printing profile (**a**) with regard to color gamut (**b**), dot gain (**c**), and color separation parameters (**d**). By comparing the color gamut of a proofing device (here, an Iris inkjet printer) to the gamut of specific offset press conditions, you can see how accurately the perceptual output from the proofing printer will match the final output.*

choose instead to convert from an RGB scanner color space directly to the final offset press color space. You can also generate an onscreen CMYK soft proof in Photoshop or QuarkXPress. And to boost productivity, FotoTune lets you create direct device-to-device conversions called *ColorLinks*, which bypass the intermediate conversion to CIE color space, thereby reducing the number of transformations and accelerating the color conversion process.

Kodak CMS Solutions

Kodak offers a continually expanding number of color management products for varying uses. Common features include the use of the term *precision transforms* to describe device color profiles and support for Photo CD color transformations. Kodak's approach is a modular one; most implementations ship with a limited number of profiles, and if you want more, you have to purchase them separately. This modular, pay-as-you-go strategy limits affordability for low-budget end users; sophisticated users can develop their own custom profiles using the PICC kit described later in this section. Kodak supports the ICC profile specification, which helps to make Kodak-generated profiles compatible with other CMSs. Most imaging professionals are already familiar with the version of KCMS supplied with Photoshop for acquiring Photo CD images. In addition to the limited version of the Kodak Color Management System (KCMS) shipped with Windows 95, here are brief summaries of some of the most notable Kodak solutions.

Kodak/DayStar ColorMatch   ColorMatch was developed jointly for Macintosh-based Photoshop and QuarkXPress users by Kodak and DayStar Digital and is now marketed by Kodak. ColorMatch includes precision transforms for Photo CD, film recorders, and a device-independent RGB color space; other precision transforms are available for monitors, flatbed and slide scanners, and color proofing devices. No offset press setup profiles are provided. ColorMatch is a little weak on monitor calibration and characterization, but you can create custom monitor profiles if you use the DayStar Digital Colorimeter 24 or any other monitor calibration device that can write to the ICC profile format. To generate a custom profile for your scanner, you need to supplement ColorMatch with Kodak's PICC kit or buy the desired profile.

Tip: *If you plan to place an image directly into a layout and don't need to edit it onscreen, you achieve the highest quality results by transforming color from the scanner or Photo CD color space directly to the color space of the final output device.*

Precision Input Color Characterization (PICC)   Kodak's Precision Input Color Characterization (PICC) module, available for both Macintosh and Windows 3.*x*, augments the capabilities of Kodak's basic Device Color Profile Starter Pack by providing a scanner calibration utility. PICC includes both a reflective and a transparent version of a standard IT8 color target. After you scan the target, PICC evaluates the accuracy of the scan and generates a precision transform for your scanner. This profile is in the same format as other precision transforms used by the Kodak Acquire module supplied with Adobe Photoshop. Place it in the KPCMS folder or directory to make it automatically available for use whenever you call up Kodak Acquire. To avoid unnecessary image degradation, it's important to apply as few color transformations during the workflow as possible.

Tip: *To calibrate and create a custom profile for Photo CD color, send Kodak's IT8 target with your photos for Photo CD processing.*

Color Management at the Operating System Level

Today's trend in CMS software is toward standardization at the operating system level. The International Color Consortium (ICC), a group made up of major software and hardware manufacturers, has developed a color profile specification that both Apple and Microsoft have adopted and implemented in their respective operating systems—Apple in ColorSync 2.0 and Microsoft in the Kodak-provided Color Management System (KCMS) incorporated into Windows 95. Any CMS requires the support of software developers to make it accessible to the end user; many hardware and software application developers have already adopted and implemented the new standards in their products.

Apple ColorSync 2

Many major device vendors and software developers have already agreed to support version 2 of ColorSync and to write ICC-compatible device profiles for it. ColorSync is also looking to the future of color printing. It supports PostScript Level 2 features, and up to eight color channels for input and output (HiFi color users, take note).

ColorSync 2 features an open architecture. It can use ICC-compliant device profiles created by other CMSs. In addition, you don't have to choose between ColorSync and a third-party CMS that you might prefer to use; if an image-editing or page layout application places a "call" to ColorSync and finds that another CMS is active in the system,

that CMS takes over to perform color transformations on an image.

Kodak Color Matching in Windows 95

Windows publishing and imaging professionals have long lamented the absence of serious color management tools on their platforms. With the advent of Windows 95, developers and device manufacturers no longer have to generate their own nonstandardized color management features.

The core of Windows 95's color management architecture, called ICM (for *Image Color Matching* framework), is integrated into monitor and printer setup routines. Windows 95 includes a core group of device profiles, which conform to the same ICC format that Apple's ColorSync also supports. For a full implementation of system-level color management to take place, however, ICM relies on the support of third-party software applications developers to call on ICM features, and on hardware device vendors to write ICC-compatible profiles.

The default color management application in Windows 95 is the Kodak Color Matching Module (similar to KCMS modules in Adobe Photoshop). Only a few profiles are supplied, but users can purchase additional profiles directly from Kodak. ICM's open architecture allows Windows 95 users to override the Kodak module and substitute another installed color management application of their choice.

PCS100 kit For high-end Macintosh imaging
and scanning applications, Kodak offers the
PCS100 kit, which includes Kodak device
profiles, a PICC-like scanner characterization
utility, a 16-bit monitor calibration device, and
an acceleration card to speed the color transform process for Photo CD and Pro Photo CD
images. With PCS100, you can also create
direct custom links between devices, which skips
the intermediate conversion to CIE color space
and saves time for each conversion. These
custom links are useful when you repeatedly
use the same scanner/monitor, scanner/printer,
or monitor/printer combination.

EfiColor Works

This low-cost CMS for Macintosh-based
QuarkXPress and Photoshop users provides an
especially large quantity of preset profiles for
proofing devices, press setup conditions, and
monitors. It supports only a small number of
scanners directly, but generating and customiz-
ing a profile for any device is an easy process
with the included scanning targets and intuitive Profile Editor. EfiColor Works' profiles are
ColorSync compliant.

For creating color separations in Photoshop,
EfiColor Works provides a large library of
Photoshop-compatible color separation tables,
all customizable. To color separate an RGB file,
you need only load the appropriate separation
table and then select CMYK from Photoshop's
Mode menu. Within QuarkXPress, you can use
the EfiColor Preferences dialog box to specify
system-wide or document-wide input and
output profiles to use when importing preseparated images from Photoshop or generating
color separations from Quark.

Among the most useful features of EfiColor
Works is the ability to fine-tune image color
management for press conditions using the Profile Editor. You can customize printer or offset
press conditions profiles with regard to transfer
functions, dot gain, and halftone settings.

Light Source Colortron

Available for both Macintosh and Windows 95
machines, the much-ballyhooed Colortron
from Light Source Computer Images, Inc.
(Figure 4–10) fills a critical niche in the color
management field. Unlike CMS software, which
can only translate color approximately
between the color spaces of different devices,
the Colortron can accurately *measure* color in
quantifiable terms. It can also translate raw
color data precisely to other color spaces, other
software programs, and even to other lighting
conditions, which makes it a perfect tool for the
exact color matching so often required in
advertising, catalog publishing, fashion photography, and commercial and interior design.

Colortron records an object's color in terms
of its raw *spectral data*—the frequency and
intensity of the light wavelengths that it
reflects. Spectral data values range from 700 nm
(*nanometers*) at the red end of the visible spectrum to 380 nm at the high frequency, violet
end. To save a color that Colortron has measured, you place it in a new or existing palette
and give it a name. Palettes are invaluable for
organizing all the colors in a project.)

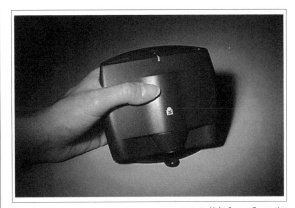

Figure 4–10   *courtesy Light Source Computing*

*The hand-held Light Source Colortron measures and
records the precise spectral data of any color, making it
useful for exact color matching through software.*

The software that accompanies Colortron is compartmentalized into several modules, each of which has specific uses in a color management context (see Figure C–6 in the Color Gallery for an overview). For example,

- The CMYK Process module displays exact CMYK equivalents based on the output color profile you designate, such as a 150-line imagesetter.

- The Colorimeter module translates a measured color precisely to its nearest equivalents in three color spaces of your choice, such as RGB, CIE Lab, or HSB.

- The Spectrum module displays all the spectral wavelengths and intensities in the current color.

- The Match module displays the closest PANTONE spot or process colors within a color difference range that you specify.

- The Lighting module shows how a given color looks under a variety of real-world lighting conditions.

- The Color Harmony module displays all the colors that are complementary to the measured color.

Tip: *Use Colortron to create a database of memory colors (apple red, grass green, flesh tones, wood and metallic textures, and so on) that you can use when editing images that require realistic color matching.*

The colors you measure with Colortron are also compatible with other software. One convenient strategy is to include all the critical colors for one project in the same palette, then import the Colortron palette (which is saved in EPS format) into a QuarkXPress or PageMaker document as a picture. All the colors in that palette immediately become part of the host document's color palette and are available for use in the page layout software. You can copy colors individually from the clipboard into Adobe Photoshop.

The Colortron can do even more than measure colors in original artwork, in ambient light, and in objects outside your computer. You can also use it as a densitometer to check the density of film. And with the optional monitor calibration device, you can calibrate your monitor and save its color characteristics in the ICC format compatible with Apple's ColorSync 2 and Windows 95 ICM. You can then use ColorSync or a third-party CMS to translate the color in the undigitized original to the monitor color space.

In this chapter, we've attempted to build a solid foundation for the color-related image-editing decisions you make when preparing images for print output. In Chapter 6 we provide guidance for generating accurate color separations, and in Chapters 7 and 8, we discuss hands-on techniques for enhancing and color-correcting images.

Image-Editing and Enhancement Tools

Before publishing found its way to the desktop, images were either stripped into a document manually or scanned using high-end proprietary systems. In either case, print communications professionals could rely on professionally photographed originals; highly trained personnel to scan, correct, and output them; and quality standards that met common industry specifications. Nowadays, you can count on none of these. The very proliferation of image sources—from RGB-generating digital cameras and desktop scanners, to amateur shots on Photo CD, to anybody-can-sell-'em stock photos of dubious pedigree—guarantees that most of what you start with isn't perfect. And to complicate matters still further, you as the end user bear the brunt of the responsibility for improving on the raw material. "Improving," for our purposes, refers to any image-editing process designed to make an image look as good in print as the original or, in some cases, better. Tonal enhancement, color correction, sharpening, retouching, and color separation all play a role in preparing an image for the printing process.

Having the hot potato of responsibility thrown into your lap is an opportunity, not a handicap. Frankly, we feel that the axiom "if you want something done right, do it yourself" applies as well to image-editing tasks as it does to home or car maintenance. The more intimately you are acquainted with the requirements of a particular print project, the more well equipped you are to understand exactly how to optimize the images that the project includes. All you then need to do is master the tools and the logistics of handling them efficiently—and that's what this chapter is about. We'll look at the "dexterity" issues of working with large image files and survey the uses of electronic tools commonly used for retouching, enhancement, and correction.

> **" *Having the hot potato of responsibility thrown into your lap is an opportunity, not a handicap.* "**

Managing Large Image Files

Whatever else you can say about digital images, one truth stands out: they just keep getting bigger. This trend is due in part to the increased use of color images in printed documents and in part to the use of larger image dimensions, as desktop professionals become more comfortable with manipulating images electronically for use in full-page ads, tabloids, spreads, and posters. (If they're getting bigger because the images are at a higher output reso-

lution than they need to be, you're wasting money and valuable storage space—see Chapters 3 and 9.) Following are a few tips and tricks to help you determine how large a file you can and should work with when performing correction and enhancement functions, and how much is just excess baggage.

Knowing When to Crop

Many graphic designers have a habit of placing an image in a page layout and then cropping it from within the layout package. Cropping a picture in a layout only reduces its visible area and doesn't crimp the file size at all; an imagesetter or platesetter still has to process the entire image during output, which can prove needlessly expensive. When in doubt, crop the image in your image-editing program before placing it. If you don't know the layout dimensions of an image in advance, try this strategy: import the entire image, finalize the design, and then crop the picture in an image-editing program, relinking the modified file to the document.

To Edit or Not to Edit in CMYK

Most digital input devices generate RGB color files; so unless you obtain all your images from drum scanners, you need to convert them to CMYK at some point before output. But when? For color images, CMYK *is* the preferred color space for performing tonal and color correction, as it more closely matches the colors that printing inks can reproduce and affords greater control over color adjustments. However, file sizes increase by one-third when you convert an RGB file to CMYK. Unless you have oodles of memory or are using a resolution-independent image-editing package like Live Picture or Macromedia xRes, it may not be necessary or even advisable to handle *all* stages of the editing process in CMYK. If you use Photoshop, you may be able to work in RGB and rely on the CMYK preview feature, as long as your system is calibrated and you've set up color separation parameters correctly (see Chapter 6). Base your decision about when to convert on a combination of workflow and system considerations.

- **System memory**—If you have enough memory to manipulate the larger CMYK file totally in RAM, by all means convert to CMYK *before* you begin the tonal and color correction process.

- **Workflow**—What do you have to do to the image before it's ready to print? If you're compositing images from multiple sources, you may need to perform subtle color and density adjustments as you go in order to critically match and merge the component elements. That would mean working in CMYK from the beginning (or, for Photoshop users, using the CMYK preview mode while working in RGB). If you're compositing images that don't require close color matching, on the other hand, there's no inherent advantage to merging images in CMYK mode. Finalize the composition in RGB and then convert before embarking on the critical tonal and color correction processes. Or, if the base image is a photograph that you plan to drop into a layout, leave the image in RGB until you've completed all local retouching tasks (removal of dust and scratch marks, elimination of facial wrinkles, and so forth) and then convert to CMYK. Figure 5–1 is a workflow diagram that you can use as a guide when determining the best time to convert from RGB to CMYK during the production process.

Tip: Photo CD images are an exception to the workflow rule, because the best time to convert them to CMYK without quality loss is when you first acquire them (see Chapter 1).

- **Press setup information**—Unless you're well informed about press type, paper stock characteristics, anticipated dot gain, recommended highlight and shadow points, and recommended ink limits at the time of conversion, and have adjusted conversion settings accordingly, RGB-to-CMYK conversion could skew color balance incorrectly and impair the output quality of your images. If you can't get to this information early in the image-editing process, leave images in the RGB color space and postpone as much tonal enhancement, color correction, and sharpening as you can until you're almost ready for output (by which time you really need to have all your ducks in a row!).

Caution: For the sake of accuracy, make sure you've calibrated your system either manually or through software before beginning any color correction process. This caveat may not apply if your color separation experience is so extensive that you feel confident doing color correction by numerical values alone.

Extra Channels and Multiple Layers

File sizes also swell when an image contains more than the standard number of channels (three for RGB, four for CMYK) or is composed of multiple layers. Let's take a look at the various forms these additions can take, just how much data they really hog, and when retaining that extra data can benefit rather than hinder the image production process.

- **Mask or alpha channels**—Leading image-editing packages allow you to save selection information either as a separate channel within the image that can be recalled, or as a separate grayscale image known as a *mask file*. These *alpha channels* or mask files let

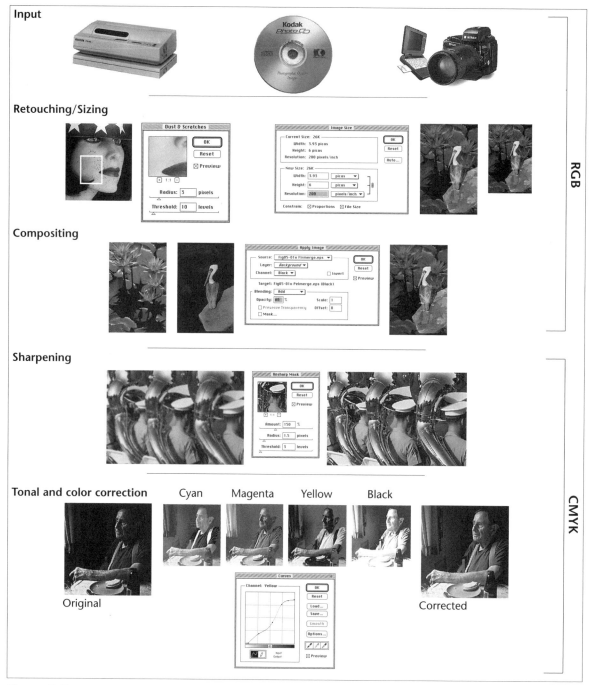

Figure 5–1

Each type of image-editing task is best handled in a specific sequence and in a particular color mode.

you quickly reselect complex areas of an image and also are useful for manipulating transparency (see Figure 5–2). In programs that save channels internally, each mask channel consumes an additional 8 bits of information over and above the base amount of data in the file, so file sizes can mount quickly if you litter an image with nonessential selections. Alpha channels are useful during the processes of retouching, compositing, and local correction, which take place most efficiently while the image is still in RGB mode. They're less essential during tonal and color correction, which are usually more effective when applied to the image as a whole rather than to individual selection areas (see Chapters 7 and 8). So for greater image-editing efficiency, put your files on a channel diet at the right time.

Tip: *If you're uncertain about whether you'll need to reuse an alpha channel, first copy it to a separate, appropriately named file and then prune the channel from the main image. Processing efficiency greatly improves as a result.*

Tip: *The caveats about masks consuming extra file space don't apply to Live Picture. It manages mask layers efficiently due to its resolution-independent FITS technology.*

- **Layers**—Useful primarily for image merging and compositing, object-oriented layers are now

© Emil Ihrig

Figure 5–2

Alpha channels used by Photoshop and other leading image editors offer a handy way to store selection information, but each one increases file size by the equivalent of a grayscale image. Saving selections as separate files rather than internal to the image can improve workflow efficiency.

available in most major image-editing programs. Layers add less data to an image file than do alpha channels; the exact amount depends on the size of the area that constitutes each layer and the opaqueness of the data in each layer. (This doesn't apply to resolution-independent programs such as Live Picture.) Compositing work is usually finished by the time you're ready for sizing, sharpening, tonal enhancement, and color correction; so in most cases it's safe to flatten the image (and reduce the file size) before performing any o f these other tasks.

- **HiFi color images**—Some color-critical print applications (high-end advertising, for example) turn to the use of more than four color plates to reproduce metallic or other special colors or to improve overall color saturation on press (see Chapter 4). HiFi color images typically consist of six or seven channels, each of which adds an additional 8 bits of data to the file. If you're a HiFi color user, you probably already have the budget and the system memory to wield the larger file sizes. In this book, we'll be concentrating on grayscale and CMYK correction techniques, but the same basic strategies also apply to HiFi color images.

Image-Enhancement Tools

Desktop-based image-editing programs are hardly kids' stuff these days. The feature sets of many leading packages rival those of closed-system, proprietary paintboxes (even if the horsepower of desktop systems lags behind). Yet only a few tools in any program are essential to the tasks involved in enhancing images professionally for print. The implementations of these tools—retouching tools, selection and masking tools, production-related filters, histograms, curves, and channels—vary slightly from one program to another, but their basic uses remain the same. We'll introduce them in the order in which they're likely to prove most useful in the prepress cycle, using Adobe Photoshop as an example.

Retouching Tools and Techniques

Defined narrowly, retouching has to do with details: the removal of undesirable details from a digital image or the addition of minor details that weren't there to begin with. When you alter an image locally to clean it up or beautify it, you're retouching. Whenever you add, subtract, or replace substantial areas of an image, you're no longer retouching—you're compositing.

Retouching is a fact of life for scanner users and for advertising and marketing professionals, but for different reasons. Lower-end and midrange flatbed scanners sometimes introduce noticeable streaks, known as *scan lines*, into a digitized image. Other types of undesirable artifacts, such as dust motes, scratches, and crimps, can appear in a scanned image due to careless handling of originals or less-than-impeccable cleanliness of the scanning device itself. Before we can attempt any creative work on a scanned image, our first task is usually to clean it up by removing these artifacts.

For designers in the advertising and marketing fields, on the other hand, the ultimate goal of retouching is to beautify an image or to make it more persuasive. To that end, it may be necessary to remove details that mar the intended effect—typical culprits being facial wrinkles, stray strands of hair, lighting glare, or other small extraneous subjects—and to add local details or highlights that enhance the effect. This type of retouching should also be taken care of before the creative processes of compositing or filtering begin.

Local Retouching Tools

Since retouching affects small areas of an image at a time, you often can accomplish it without the help of selection areas or masks, using only the local enhancement tools found in the toolbox of your image-editing package.

Here's an overview of the most commonly used types of retouching tools and the functions of each:

- *Cloning tools* work by copying details from one area of an image to another. In cases of scan lines, dust marks, and scratches, use cloning tools to replace the scanning artifacts with tones and details from similarly colored, more perfect areas of the same or another image. You can also use tools of this type to "erase" subjects that occur naturally in an image but are undesirable in the final product. When your main goal is to enhance an image that's already acceptable, cloning tools can increase the number of flowers in a vase, thicken eyelashes, and otherwise intensify the emotional impact of the picture. Careful attention to tonal similarity between the source and destination areas is necessary to ensure that retouched areas continue to look natural.

- *Smudge and smear tools* blend and smooth the differences between adjacent tones wherever the brush passes. They're useful for eliminating wrinkles, crease lines in clothing, random scanner noise, and the like. An airbrush tool can often achieve similar effects.

- *Sharpening and blurring tools* allow you to increase or decrease contrast locally on a pixel-by-pixel basis. Local sharpening can intensify the sparkle of jewelry or draw more attention to key subject areas. Local blurring tones down undesirable features, dulls insignificant details, and helps distract attention from unimportant subjects.

- *Lightening and darkening tools* brighten or dim subjects locally. They're useful for correcting inconsistent lighting and for manipulating brightness values to emphasize or de-emphasize specific details.

Tip: Pay careful attention to brush size, brush opacity, and anti-aliasing settings when using the retouching tools to avoid a clumsy, artificial look in retouched areas. For example, use a hard clone brush when retouching an area where the grain in the surrounding area is sharp; a feathered clone brush would soften the grain and produce an unnatural-looking effect. And when retouching extremely fine details, magnify the image many times to ensure accuracy.

Filters for Retouching

Most filters cater to the tastes of special-effects aficionados, but some truly aid in production tasks. When used in conjunction with selected areas or masks (see "Tools for Selective Enhancement," following), a few filters can also perform retouching functions. The most useful types of filters for retouching purposes are

- **Unsharp masking and edge-sharpening filters**—These filters heighten contrast and detail. When applied locally for retouching purposes, they help emphasize some details over others.

- **Blurring and softening filters**—These are useful for de-emphasizing and eliminating scanner artifacts and smoothing away minor, unwanted details.

- **Noise-inducing filters**—Adding random noise to a small selected area helps cover up minor artifacts or unsightly features.

- **Despeckling filters**—Despeckling-type filters (a category that also includes Median and Photoshop's Dust & Scratches, for example) remove scanner artifacts and help eliminate unsightly details in high-contrast areas of faces and other important subject matter. Despeckling filters can soften affected areas, so it's often useful to follow up with an application of a sharpening filter.

Tools for Selective Enhancement

Tonal correction, color correction, and sharpening are usually most effective when you apply them to an image as a whole. For retouching operations, local, freehand work is the rule of thumb. But some image-editing tasks require *selective enhancement*—isolating one part of an image in order to manipulate it separately from the whole. For example, you might choose to increase definition, alter brightness levels, or intensify color saturation in one subject area only, in order to better communicate your message. For such tasks, you need the help of selection and masking tools and/or layers.

Selection and Masking Tools

The terms *selection* and *mask* are often used interchangeably, but there's a minor yet significant difference between them. Selections are temporary, while masks are basically selection areas that have been saved digitally for ease of future retrieval. If you plan on manipulating the information in an isolated area of an image only once, then a temporary selection will do the job. But if the selection area is complex and you suspect that you'll need to alter the information in it multiple times during the course of a project, by all means save the information as a mask. Some image-editing programs allow you to save each mask as a separate channel within the main file, while others require that you store mask information in separate files. The latter option places no extra burden on file size.

Isolating part of an image can be a time-consuming or otherwise difficult task, especially if the area has a complex shape or is defined by color rather than shape. That's where selection tools step in to ease the job. Most image-editing applications offer at least the following three or four basic types of tools for defining selections and masks (see Figure 5–3 for a visual reference). Using these types of tools singly or in combination to add to or subtract from a selection area, you can select almost any portion of an image automatically.

- *Geometrical selection tools* let you select areas that have a rectangular, square, elliptical, or circular shape. Not many subjects have such simple shapes! Geometrical tools are at their most handy when you need to use multiple selection tools to build up a complex selection that has some geometrical components (the front face of a camera, for instance).

- *Freehand selection tools*, such as the familiar Lasso tool, allow you to trace around a complex shape in order to select it. Novice Lasso users often try to trace a very complex area in one sweep with the mouse button continuously depressed, which can yield frustrating results for anyone whose hand is less than rock-steady. You can trace complex shapes much more accurately by zooming in on the area and then clicking at every point where the shape begins to curve slightly.

- *Path tools* work in a manner similar to Lasso-type tools, except that they generate vector objects from the areas you select. Vector objects have several advantages over ordinary selections: they take up less file space; they can be imported to drawing programs such as Adobe Illustrator, Macromedia FreeHand, and CorelDRAW!; they can be scaled without quality loss; and they are composed of *control points* that you can drag to manipulate the path's shape precisely. Depending on the program, you may be able to convert a path to a normal selection.

- *Color range selection tools*, often called magic wands, select image information based on the similarity between adjacent colors. The color on which you click helps to control the size and shape of the selection area; so does the color similarity range you define. Defining the appropriate color similarity range and obtaining accurate selections

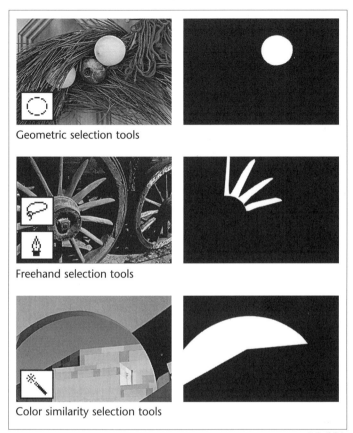

Geometric selection tools

Freehand selection tools

Color similarity selection tools

Figure 5–3

© Emil Ihrig

Standard selection tools isolate image information based on geometrical shapes, complex shapes traced freehand, or color similarity range.

takes practice and the help of a densitometer or eye-dropper tool for surveying the color values in the desired selection area. Often, the use of multiple selection tools is necessary to continue building a selection that the color similarity tool couldn't complete.

Tip: *When selecting a complex area, use more than one type of tool if necessary to subtract from or add to the selection. Also use feathering when selecting hair and other delicate areas so that the effects you apply are subtle and your final composition doesn't look artificial.*

Using Layers

Increasingly, image-editing packages are supporting the use of multiple object-oriented layers. Layers are useful primarily for creative processes such as image compositing, because data in any given layer is completely independent of all others and can therefore be moved and manipulated at will. By the time you're ready for the production-oriented tasks we describe in this book, you should ideally have completed the creative phase of the project, and so you'll usually work with "flattened" images that have been merged into a single layer. However, we mention layers here because they do offer another method for isolating data in an image, and because creative and production schedules in hectic environments sometimes get compressed and overlap.

If you do perform tonal adjustment, color correction, sharpening, or other production tasks on a multilayered image, keep in mind that your adjustments apply only to the currently active layer. Take care to adjust all layers in a consistent way, except for those layers where only local enhancement is desired (changing the color of a model's dress in a clothing catalog, for example).

Histograms

Histograms like the ones shown in Figure 5–4 are an essential reference tool for all tonal adjustment, color correction, and sharpening tasks. They provide an at-a-glance visual graph of the distribution of tones in an image. The horizontal axis of a

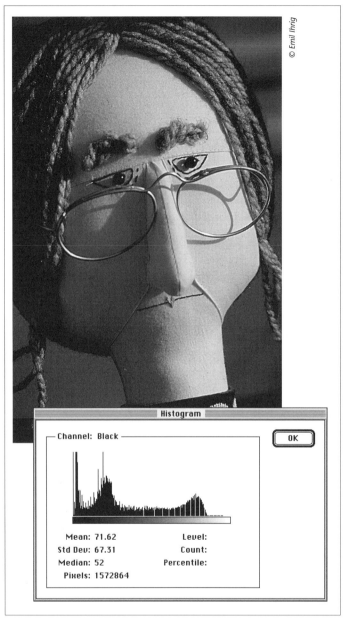

Histogram

Channel: Black

OK

Mean: 71.62   Level:
Std Dev: 67.31   Count:
Median: 52   Percentile:
Pixels: 1572864

© Emil Ihrig

Figure 5–4

*Histograms visually map the distribution of brightness levels in an image
or of separate channels in an image and can therefore serve as an
excellent guide to determining a tonal and color correction strategy. The
histogram for this image, for example, shows obvious peaks in the
darkest and lightest portions of the tonal range and is therefore
indicative of high contrast levels.*

histogram maps the available brightness levels from dark (left) to light (right), while the vertical axis indicates the relative proportion of pixels in the image assigned to each brightness level.

By reviewing the histogram for an image prior to beginning the enhancement and correction process, you can determine which tonal and color ranges require adjustment for printing and develop a clear strategy for exactly *how* to adjust them. The histogram of an unaltered image, for example, tells you whether the digitizing device was able to capture all the tones available in the undigitized original—vertical breaks or gaps in what should otherwise be a smooth tonal continuum indicate that the scanner couldn't quite cut the mustard, resulting in a quality loss. A histogram shows whether the image as a whole is too bright, too dark, or just right, and which levels of brightness contain the greatest amount of detail. It also reveals which tonal or color ranges require more contrast and which ones could stand to flatten out a little without quality loss. Most programs also let you view separate histograms for each color channel, which can help you to fine-tune adjustments even more precisely.

If your scanner can't capture all the tones in most originals, you don't necessarily have to junk it. Print media can't reproduce all the tones in a photographic-quality original anyway, so eventual output quality depends largely on your ability to make the best of what's available. You can still obtain good print quality with less than perfect input if you understand the principles of image correction described in Chapters 6 through 8.

Densitometer Tools

The relationship between a histogram and an eyedropper or densitometer tool is like the relationship between a statistical report and an interview: the report describes the general trends, but only an interview can ferret out what's happening to individual people on a day-to-day level. In the same way, a histogram describes which general tonal ranges need help, but only a pixel-by-pixel survey of an image with an eyedropper can tell you exactly which subject areas are affected. Densitometer tools help you to pinpoint the lightest and darkest subjects in an image and determine whether these need to be adjusted before printing. They also can clue you in to whether color imbalances exist in important subject areas and how best to compensate for them.

Curves

Curves are undoubtedly the most powerful and sophisticated tools for adjusting tone, color, and sharpness in a digital image. High-end paintbox systems and top-of-the-line scanners have long used them to prepare images for print, and mainstream image-editing packages are increasingly following their lead. Together, histograms, densitometer tools, and curves can fulfill most of your prepress needs: use a histogram to provide a general overview of an image's potential, an eyedropper tool to obtain a pinpointed diagnosis, and curve-based adjustments to apply the remedy.

A phenomenon known as *tonal compression* necessarily takes place when images are to be reproduced in print. Paper and ink simply can't reproduce the full range of tones and colors from black to white, no matter how high-end a

scanner or camera captured the image to begin with. (Of course, higher grades of paper do a better job than lower grades.) In the interest of salvaging as much contrast and detail as possible, you must first compress the available tones into a narrower range and then juggle what's left. Curves allow us to perform this juggling act expertly and intuitively (see Figure 5–5).

Figure 5–5   © Emil Ihrig

*Editing the tonal and color ranges represented by a curve is like manipulating a rubber band: as you stretch one segment of the rubber band, another segment contracts. The art of prepress enhancement is one of making the right choices about which segments to stretch. Here, the original image (**top**) lacks contrast in the lighter subject areas (the components of the flowers) and between the flowers and the background objects. Flattening the curve in the lightest ranges and steepening it in moderately bright areas (**center**) strengthens the available detail in the flowers. Flattening the curve in the medium-to-dark range (which contains the less important subjects) makes the flowers stand out against the lily pads (**bottom**).*

Curves are basically a tool for altering contrast relationships in many brightness ranges of an image at once. A default, unaltered curve is a straight line at a 45-degree angle, showing a linear progression of brightness levels from light to dark. As you edit the curve, you are altering the final (output) brightness levels relative to that original (input) straight line. It's all about brightness and contrast. Wherever you steepen the curve, you introduce a wider range of colors or tones into corresponding subject areas of the image, and the image gains in contrast and apparent detail. Wherever you flatten the curve to less than a 45-degree angle, you compress the color range and the amount of contrast. There are only so many brightness levels available, and this fact gives the curve adjustment process something of the character of a rubber band: if you stretch one section of the rubber band, another section necessarily becomes taut. The art of prepress enhancement and correction is therefore largely one of making the right choices about which segments of the rubber band to stretch and which you can allow to tighten. As you'll see again in Chapters 7 and 8, the subject matter of an image and your intended message can guide you to the correct decisions. Channels also come into play to help you with this process. For color images, you can edit curves for the composite image or separately for each channel.

Our aim in this chapter has been to provide an overview of the tools that will help you most in correcting and enhancing images, and to offer guidance about the logistics of doing so efficiently. In the next few chapters, we'll lay out a series of more detailed road maps for the processes of color separation, tonal and color correction, sharpening, and other common prepress tasks.

Color *Separations* and *Conversions*

6

T hose of us who work in print media normally output full-color images in CMYK, black-and-white images in grayscale, and tinted images in spot color. Yet, more often than not, digital images come to us in a color mode other than the one we need for final output. For example:

- Digital cameras, flatbed and slide scanners, and Photo CD workstations digitize color in RGB rather than in CMYK;
- We receive scans or Photo CD images in color, but have to print them in black and white; or
- The design concepts for a publication suddenly change in midstream.

The result is that conversions between color modes become an integral part of our everyday image-editing procedures.

The art of conversion, while not always as creative as some other production tasks, is nevertheless one worth mastering. The way an image translates from one color mode to another determines much about the raw quality of the resulting file. If you take a slapdash attitude toward this important process, your images could sacrifice valuable contrast and detail, or contain color imbalances that make life difficult for press operators.

Note: *Correcting for unsatisfactory color separations on press is inadvisable. Not only is it difficult to make even subtle changes, but it also results in inferior jobs.*

In this chapter, we provide guidelines for three types of color conversions that designers and other print communications professionals commonly encounter:

- Conversions from RGB to CMYK (color separations)

- Conversions from color to grayscale

- Conversions from color or black and white to tints or duotones

Granted, conversion is only a first step in preparing an image for print output. But converting correctly, with the proper preparation and software settings, provides you with the quality raw material you need to polish the final artwork without having to perform unnecessary acrobatics. It makes your later image-editing work so much easier!

Color Separation Decisions

Many people regard professional color separators as graphic arts rocket scientists who ply their arcane knowledge high above the intellectual horizons of mere mortals. But, surprise: every time you translate an image from RGB, LAB, or HSB into CMYK, you're an instant color separator. Final color correction is most effective when you perform it in the CMYK color space (see Chapter 8), so you owe it to the quality of your printed images to know how to get there by the most efficient route possible. Setting the wrong parameters for translating a file to the CMYK mode can make it difficult for the designer, the color prepress professional,

and the press operator to obtain believable color, crisp detail, and proper contrast in the final printed piece.

"Every time you translate an image from RGB, LAB, or HSB into CMYK, you're an instant color separator."

Although you'll find many noodles in this alphabet soup, much of the hoopla surrounding the art and science of color separation boils down to just a few basic issues. How much ink should be placed on a page? How much of that ink should be black ink? And how can you juggle the CMYK balance to obtain the most lifelike colors using the least amount of ink?

The field of color separation has its own jargon, common elements of which appear in most major image-editing packages. The remainder of this section consists of a brief rundown of the most important terms and acronyms you'll encounter, along with general guidelines for applying each parameter. First, though, let's consider a basic rule of the game for translating a file into CMYK.

Avoid Multiple Conversions

Desktop scans, Photo CD images, and captures from digital cameras come to you in the RGB color space. There may be times when you're performing other tasks that require you to work continuously in RGB, or when you don't have enough information from your print vendor to create a separation before beginning color and tonal correction. In these cases, let the image remain in RGB as long as possible, and take advantage of the CMYK preview mode that many major imaging packages support.

If you're unsure of yourself when creating color separations, a good strategy is to generate the separation based on a duplicate of the original, so that you can backtrack easily. If for some unforeseen reason you need to return from CMYK to the RGB color space temporarily and you're using Adobe Photoshop, you can do so safely by transferring into the CIELAB color space as an intermediate step. But don't do this more than once. Quality loss is inevitable with multiple conversions. Once translated, the original RGB colors are impossible to reconstruct (even when you transfer to and from the CIELAB mode), because colors outside of the CMYK gamut have been thrown away permanently.

Tip: *Some color management software vendors provide ready-made or customizable color conversion profiles based on known characteristics of a final output device or press type. Agfa and Eastman Kodak are among the best-known vendors of such output device profiles.*

Total Ink Coverage

Each of the CMYK inks can have values ranging from 0 to 100 percent. Adding up each of the CMYK values for a given pixel tells you what total percentage of ink (the *total ink coverage*) will be applied to paper at that point on the page. A pixel with the values 67C54M53Y72K, for example, represents a total ink coverage of $67 + 54 + 53 + 72 = 246$ percent, equivalent to a 90 percent gray to the human eye.

There's nothing to prevent you from assigning total ink coverages of 400 percent (or 100 percent for each component color) to some areas of an image, but your print vendor probably would divorce you if you did. The reasons have to do with the interaction of paper and ink on press. Process color printing requires that inks be applied to the same sheet of paper four different times. Most inks in commercial use are wet! And just as you might expect,

every time you add more wetness (more ink) to a sheet of paper, colors spread and contaminate each other's spaces more and more, much like when you allow water to leach into a paper towel. So the wetter you make the blend, the more desperate the dot gain situation becomes, until any hopes you had of detail in darker areas dissolve into a plugged-up, undifferentiated black.

Total Ink Limit

The only way to preserve detail in darker areas of a printed color image, then, is to limit the total percentage of ink that can be applied to the paper—hence the term *total ink limit*. The total ink limit advisable for a given project depends on press type, press speed, and the characteristics of the paper stock. Projects that will be printed on high-speed web offset presses using cheaper, more absorbent grades of paper (uncoated stocks or newsprint) have a relatively low recommended total ink limit. Allowable total ink limits are higher for sheet-fed presses and for quality coated paper stocks that don't absorb ink excessively. Lower total ink limits present special challenges to managing the black channel, as we'll see shortly.

SWOP to the Rescue

Just how high a total ink limit should you assign for a given project and paper stock? If you'll be printing to a web offset or rotogravure press (as many advertisements, magazines, catalogs, books, and other medium- to high-volume commercial documents do), a set of standards called *SWOP* (for *Specifications for Web Offset Publications*) can guide you. First developed in the 1970s by the magazine and catalog industry, SWOP standards are updated every few years. SWOP 1993 recommends a maximum total ink limit of 300 percent, with no more than one color printing at 100 percent. In practice, many professionals in the advertising, magazine, and catalog fields drop the total ink limit even lower, to 280 percent, and if lesser-quality paper is used, to about 260 percent. On the other hand, sheet-fed color documents on coated stock can sometimes take maximum ink densities of 320 or 330, especially if the print vendor uses a waterless press.

One consequence of limiting ink coverage severely is that it becomes much more difficult to reproduce intense colors. Many of the digital acrobatics that professional color separators perform on individual color channels aim at overcoming this deficiency. The HiFi color movement (see Chapter 4) has its own solution to the problem—use additional channels and a different ink set, and achieve more brilliant colors with less ink coverage.

Note: *SWOP ink limit standards don't necessarily apply to newspapers, brochures, fine art books, art reproductions, commercial packaging, or other documents printed on newspaper, sheet-fed, or flexographic presses. Industry standards are hard to come by for these press types because setups can vary so widely. If your projects fall outside the SWOP domain, make sure your print vendor has extensive experience in your document type and consult the vendor for specific recommendations.*

Managing the Black Channel

As we've seen in earlier chapters, inherent ink impurities (particularly in cyan inks) present a challenge to obtaining vivid blues and greens on press. Ink coverage restraints present a further challenge to reproducing *any* lifelike colors: as total ink limit *decreases*, the proportion of black relative to the other colors in a separation *increases*, making it correspondingly more difficult to get brilliant colors. The situation is serious, but not hopeless. One of your most powerful tools for remedying these deficiencies

is the black (K) channel. When generated properly at the time of converting to the CMYK color space, the black channel can help define detail in shadows and in transitional areas wherever contrast occurs. Crisper detail and beefed-up contrast enhance the *appearance* of saturation and can thus fool the eye into seeing colors as more brilliant than they actually are.

Images separated using CMY inks alone can lack contrast and appear hazy, especially in transitional and shadow areas. (This is particularly the case with high-contrast, extremely colorful images.) When separated using a fourth, black channel, the same images appear sharper and their colors more lively, thanks to the contouring effect that black provides.

However, simply adding black isn't enough to guarantee perfect color. For truly professional results, you need to concern yourself with how *much* black to add, where to add it, and how best to balance the distribution of ink between black and the other channels. You address these issue when you make decisions about black generation amount, black ink limits, GCR, UCR, and UCA.

Black Generation

Press operators have some control over the amounts and mixture of inks they allow onto your pages; so even if your work is less than perfect, they have leeway to do damage control. You can give them even more leeway if your black plate isn't excessively heavy to begin with.

If you're creating a GCR type of color separation, you can specify a *black generation* amount in Photoshop and other leading image-editing packages. Black generation amount determines the total amount of black in an image *relative* to the other three color plates. For most types of images, a Light setting is preferable and is equivalent to what printers traditionally have referred to as a *skeleton black*—just enough black to add contour and to emphasize contrast and detail. If in the course of color correction you ever need to increase black values in an image, starting with a skeleton black will give you room to maneuver without muddying up other colors. Figure 6–1 shows how the black plate for the image in Figure C–7 changes when you vary the amount of black generation.

Tip: *Total ink limit remains fixed, regardless of whether you use three color plates or four. So when you intensify the black plate, you necessarily rob color from the other three.*

Image content and output parameters can help you determine how much black generation is desirable. Here are some general guidelines.

Low-key and high-key images

Generate a light or skeleton black for low-key images such as night scenes, and for high-key images in which all the details are light. In night scenes, you'll want to preserve as much color and detail as possible, and these will go by the wayside if the black plate is too heavy. The human eye doesn't perceive color imbalances easily in shadow areas, so it's all right to leave low-key images predominantly CMY. High-key images can easily become muddy and grainy if you allow more than a touch of black to seep in.

Images with neutral subject

matter Images whose main subject matter consists of neutral colors or metallics—city buildings or coins, for example—can benefit from medium or even heavy black generation (see Figure 6–2 and Figure C–8 in the Color Gallery). When neutrals (particularly lighter neutrals) are the

Light black generation

Medium black generation

Heavy black generation

Maximum black generation

Figure 6–1   © Emil Ihrig

The black generation amount controls how heavy the black plate prints relative to the other ink colors. Note the subtle increase in contrast and detail of the black plate as the amount is increased. The Medium black plate is the one used for the image in Figure C–7.

center of attention, avoiding color casts is a high priority. Increasing the amount of black in the image helps ensure a higher neutral content for the overall color makeup.

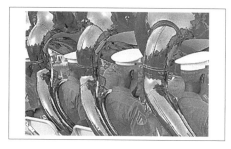

Figure 6–2

© Emil Ihrig

Images that emphasize predominantly grayscale or metallic subjects, such as the military band photo in Figure C–8, separate best using heavier amounts of black, which help prevent the introduction of color casts on press. **Top to bottom:** *the cyan, magenta, yellow, and black plates for a predominantly neutral image separated using heavy black generation.*

Press setup and quality control If your project requires a total ink limit of 280 or lower, your separations will automatically have a high black content relative to the other colors. Specifying a heavy amount of black is therefore not advisable unless the subject matter of an image dictates it. Also, if you know from past experience that the print vendor for a given project tends to overdo the black, keep black generation to a minimum.

Risk of misregistration Documents printed on high-speed web offset or rotogravure presses are more prone to misregistration than are documents printed on slower sheet-fed presses. The results of misregistration, though, are less obvious when it occurs on the black plate than when it occurs on one of the other color plates. Medium to heavy black generation may therefore be acceptable for some images that are printed on higher-speed presses.

Black Ink Limit

In many image-editing packages, simply determining how much black to add to an image overall isn't enough; you also need to specify the darkest permitted black value, known as the *black ink limit*. Press and paper parameters cause this value to vary from project to project, but typical values fall between 70 and 90 percent—near the lower value for lesser-quality papers (such as newsprint) and higher-speed presses, and near the higher value for coated stocks printed on sheet-fed presses. For example, in an image printing on coated stock on a web offset press (assuming a total ink limit of 300), the darkest shadow value that still contains visible detail falls at approximately 80C70M70Y70K; darker values will print as black.

Tip: *Many variables—such as the use of a varnish coat and the order in which color plates are printed—contribute to setting the values for the black ink limit and the darkest perceptible printed color. The highest-quality coated stocks can take a black ink limit of 100 percent; brochures printed on 80-pound coated text stock typically use a black ink limit of 90 percent.*

The Alphabet Soup: GCR, UCA, and UCR

The tonal ranges in which black will appear are just as important as the amount of black generated and the darkest permitted value of black. The acronyms in the alphabet soup of color separation—GCR, UCA, and UCR—all address this issue in different ways. All three help to solve the problems of preserving detail and contrast without incurring excess ink coverage.

GCR: replacing neutrals with black

The initials in the acronym GCR (for *gray component replacement*) have two generally accepted meanings. One derives from the theory that in any color, two of the CMY colors predominate and determine the hue, while the third color, called the *gray component* or the *unwanted color*, fulfills the function of black, darkening and *killing* the hue if too much is added. Red, for example, contains mostly magenta and yellow and becomes dirty if you add more than a small amount of cyan to it; where red is concerned, cyan is the gray component color. The term "gray component" also can refer to the roughly equal amounts of cyan, magenta, and yellow *within* a color that together make up a neutral gray. Black can safely be substituted for the neutral or gray component of a color.

In GCR separations, the appropriate amount of black replaces the unwanted color or the neutral gray component. This strategy reduces total ink coverage because black darkens a color three times as much as an equivalent amount of cyan, magenta, or yellow. Using black to replace other colors has the added advantage of reducing the risk of color casts, especially where known colors such as flesh tones, fresh produce, metallics, or sky predominate.

In a typical GCR separation where UCA is *not* used, black helps keep colors crisp by dominating transitional areas where contouring is most important. Black can appear throughout the tonal range, beginning to replace other ink colors as soon as the total coverage of cyan, magenta, and yellow exceed about 100 percent. The amount of black builds gradually and then increases sharply in the shadow tones, where the eye can't distinguish easily between colors and neutrals. Images that need to remain richly colorful in all tonal ranges—light, medium, and dark—are therefore the best candidates for GCR separations.

UCA: retaining color saturation in the shadows

GCR is the preferred method of color separation in use today, but it has its disadvantages: shadow tones can lack detail, and blacks can appear flat. These problems are especially obvious in low-key images, which are composed predominantly of darker colors.

Printing industry professionals know that four-color (CMYK) blacks and shadows look richer than equivalent colors created predominantly or solely with black. To preserve color saturation and depth in the shadow tones of GCR separations, they have devised a technique known as *UCA* (short for *undercolor addition*), which removes some black from darker colors and reintroduces cyan, magenta, and yellow in its place. The higher the amount of UCA you specify in a GCR separation, the more shadow black you'll replace with CMY. Figure 6–3 shows an example of GCR used with UCA.

Apply UCA to night scenes, to low-key images in general, to Rembrandt-like pictures that contain richly colorful midtones adjacent to contrasting shadow areas, and to documents that will be printed with a varnish coat. Avoid UCA on images in which neutral subjects predominate. And, since UCA increases rather than reduces ink coverage in the shadow tones, it's safest when your allowable ink limit is relatively high and when you'll be printing to less-absorbent paper stocks. Ask your print vendor for recommendations.

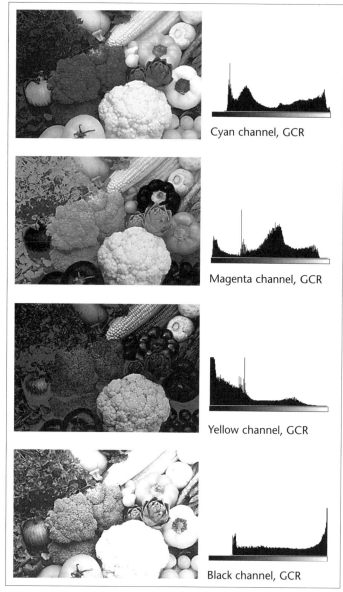

Cyan channel, GCR

Magenta channel, GCR

Yellow channel, GCR

Black channel, GCR

Figure 6–3

courtesy MetaTools, Inc. (KPT PowerPhotos)

The still life in Figure C–9 is a good candidate for a GCR/UCA separa-tion. It contains a broad spectrum of colors that are rich and saturated in all tonal ranges. Here, the component channels of the image and their accompanying histograms graphically demonstrate a typical distribution of colors in GCR-separated images where UCA is also used. Black can appear in all tonal ranges, but in the shadow tones, the other three colors predominate to produce a richer look. In a GCR-only separation, the black channel would show heavier coverage in the shadows.

Tip: *Reintroducing color in the shadow tones involves no significant risk for color casts—the eye is less sensitive to color casts in darker tones than in lighter ones.*

UCR: deepening the shadows

Whereas GCR substitutes black for CMY neutrals in any tonal range, *UCR* (for *undercolor removal*) substitutes it only in darker areas where black is already printing. As Figure C–10 in the Color Gallery and Figure 6–4 show, that means little or no black in the highlights, a small amount in the midtones, and a whole lot more in the shadows. UCR is a long-established technique for reducing total ink coverage in shadows while enhancing detail. It's most useful for images that will be printed on high-speed presses using uncoated stocks—conditions in which brief ink drying times could cause darker details to plug up. UCR's main drawback is that dark tones can appear flat and lacking in contrast, which is why it yields the best results for images that contain predominantly neutral subjects in the darker tones. When images feature colorful midtones and shadows, on the other hand, avoid UCR; use GCR with UCA instead.

Setting Paper and Ink Parameters

An additional factor that influences how color values convert from RGB to CMYK is the *press setup*—the com-bination of press type, ink set, and paper stock used for the final print job. In some programs you set each parameter separately; in others (such as Photoshop's Printing Inks Setup dialog box), certain combinations of paper stocks and ink sets assume a specific press or printer type.

Choosing an Ink Set

Always ask your print vendor what kinds of inks will be used for a particular job (SWOP and Toyo are common for offset printing). Specifying the correct ink set is particularly important, since the *gray balance*, or relative amount of each CMY pigment required to reproduce a neutral grayscale without color cast, varies from one ink set to another. See the "Gray Balance: Neutral Is Not Equal" sidebar for an example of how a neutral grayscale converts to CMYK based on a specific set of color separation parameters.

Tip: *If exact information about ink sets is unavailable to you, you can obtain good results by visually calibrating your system to a contract-quality proof of an image (see Chapter 4) and then visually adjusting each image in a publication using tone curves.*

Paper Stock and Dot Gain

Paper stock affects many aspects of a print job, but the one you should be most concerned with when making a color separation is the amount of dot gain. As a general rule, coated papers evidence the lowest amount of dot gain because they're the least absorbent stocks. Uncoated papers are subject to a higher amount, and newsprint is the worst culprit of all.

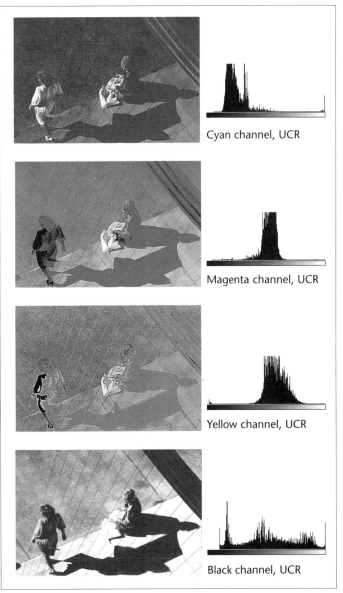

Cyan channel, UCR

Magenta channel, UCR

Yellow channel, UCR

Black channel, UCR

Figure 6–4   © Emil Ihrig

Images with neutral or near-neutral subjects in the midtones and shadows, such as the example in Figure C–10 in the Color Gallery, are excellent candidates for UCR separations. As these component channels and their histograms show, the darker tones in a UCR separation are composed predominantly of black, which helps prevent color casts in those darker neutral subjects. UCR is also useful when the total ink limit for a project is 260 percent or lower; although it may flatten the richness of darker colors, it prevents ink saturation problems on press.

Gray Balance: Neutral Is Not Equal

If you convert a stepped grayscale like the one in Figure 6–5 to CMYK and then check the CMYK values of each step, you'll notice that the cyan value is always higher than the magenta and yellow values, which are roughly equal to one another. These seemingly strange numbers indicate that the *gray balance*—the amount of each color required to produce a true neutral gray—demands a shift toward cyan. This shift is not accidental; as explained in Chapter 4, inherent impurities in cyan ink require that it print heavier than magenta and yellow in order to reproduce a neutral accurately. The exact amount of difference between cyan and the other two primaries depends on the portion of the tonal range you're examining and the color separation parameters you've chosen. Typically, the gap between cyan and the other colors is smallest in the highlights, increases to its maximum in the midtones, and tapers off just slightly toward the shadows.

Note: *Black generation and black ink limit settings directly impact the balance between cyan and other colors in a color separated image, particularly in the darker tones.*

When you're setting highlight and shadow values or performing color correction, it's important to be familiar with the CMY gray balance differences for your project in all portions of the tonal range, especially at the highlight and shadow points. Knowing these values can help you spot and correct for color casts whenever neutral grays appear in an image. However, if you work on multiple print projects with different color separation parameters or have other work responsibilities in addition to image editing, you probably can't be bothered with memorizing the values. Here's an easy system that you can use with any project to provide yourself with a handy visual reminder that you can reach for at any time:

1. Obtain the correct color separation parameters for the project from your print vendor. Ask for the highlight and shadow values, the total and black ink limits, the ink set and paper stock characteristics, the type of separation (GCR or UCR), and (if GCR is to be used) the best amount of UCA to specify.

2. In your image-editing package, create a stepped graysale large enough to contain tonal blocks in all of the following increments: the printer-specified highlight value, 5%, 10%, 20%, 25% (quartertone), 30%, 40%, 50% (midtone), 60%, 70%, 75% (three-quartertone), 80%, 90%, printer-specified shadow value, 95%, and 100%. (The 5% and 95% patches improve accuracy, since those are the tones at which many imagesetters lose control over subtle detail.) Arrange the blocks vertically in the order of lightest to darkest.

3. Enter the printer-specified color separation parameters for your project.

4. Convert the stepped grayscale to CMYK using the above parameters.

5. Print the grayscale.

6. Using an eyedropper or onscreen densitometer tool, check the CMYK values of each grayscale block and write them

down next to the appropriate block on the printed version. Use this chart for reference during the tonal and color correction process.

Figure 6–5 and Table 6–1 offer an example of this type of chart for a particular set of color separation parameters. In our case, we assumed a printer-recommended highlight value of 4 percent and a shadow value of 96 percent—parameters that may be quite different for your projects. We specified SWOP inks, coated stock, GCR separation with light black generation, a total ink limit of 300 percent, a black ink limit of 85 percent, and no UCA. The variations between cyan and the other colors would be greater if we had requested a lower total ink limit. See Chapter 7 for information about the importance of highlights, shadows, and other parts of the tonal range.

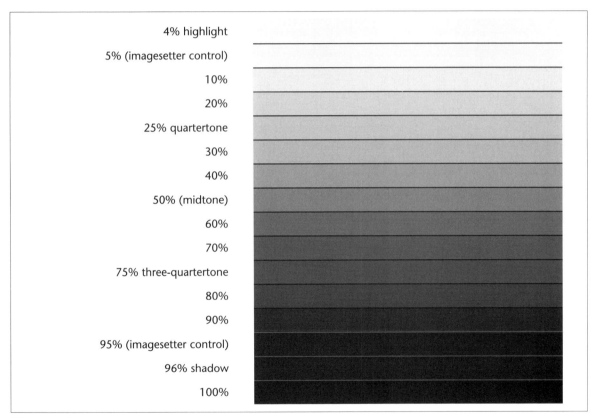

Figure 6–5

By comparing the grayscale and CMYK versions of a stepped grayscale like this one (see the "Gray Balance: Neutral is Not Equal" sidebar), you can see why grays require higher amounts of cyan than magenta and yellow in order to print as truly neutral. The amount of variance between cyan and the other ink colors varies with each part of the tonal range and depends on the color separation parameters for a particular image or project.

Grayscale Value (%)	Cyan	Magenta	Yellow	Black	Cyan Difference
4%	3	2	2	0	1% highlight
5%	4	2	3	0	1–2%
10%	8	5	5	0	3%
20%	17	11	11	0	6%
25%	22	14	14	0	8% quartertone
30%	26	17	17	0	9%
40%	35	24	24	0	11%
50%	44	31	31	1	13% midtone
60%	53	40	39	3	13%
70%	62	48	47	9	14%
75%	65	53	51	14	12–14% three-quartertone
80%	69	57	56	21	12–13%
90%	78	67	66	43	11–12%
95%	79	68	67	59	11–12%
96%	79	68	67	65	11–12% shadow
100%	79	68	67	85	11–12%

Table 6–1

This chart shows gray balance differences between cyan and magenta/yellow for each part of the tonal range. The color separation parameters that yield these values are GCR separation, light black generation, total ink limit of 300 percent, black ink limit of 96 percent, and no UCA. Printer highlight and shadow limits of 4 percent and 96 percent are assumed.

But there's a wide range of variation in dot gain, even within a paper type—get recommendations from your print vendor for the specific stock selected for each job.

Dot gain is heaviest in the midtones and shadows (the medium-to-dark subject areas). In North America, dot gain is measured at the 50 percent dot; whereas in Europe, both the 40 and 80 percent dots are measured. When you request dot gain information, keep in mind that print vendors may quote dot gain in differ-

ent ways. Press professionals who got into the business before the advent of desktop publishing specify dot gain in relative terms, as a percentage of the 50 percent dot. To these "old-timers," a 20 percent dot gain means that a 50 percent dot prints as 60 percent (50 percent plus 20 percent of 50 percent = 50 + 10 percent = 60 percent). To those weaned on electronics, on the other hand, dot gain is an absolute value: a 20 percent dot gain means that the 50 percent dot prints as a 70 percent dot (a straight-

Figure C–1

"Access Denied"
by Emil Ihrig

When print projects are to contain original raster illustrations or montages created entirely in paint or image-editing software, as in this example, the artist should be advised of the correct print dimensions and output resolution before any creative work begins. Artwork can then be created at the proper size and resolution for final output so that later compromises to image quality are not necessary.

© Emil Ihrig

Figure C–2

In process-color printing, each of the four CMYK plates prints at a different angle, forming a rosette of dots. Traditionally, dots in the cyan plate print at 105 degrees, in the magenta plate at 75 degrees, in the yellow plate at 0 or 90 degrees, and in the black plate at 45 degrees. (Many current digital technologies adjust these angles slightly to prevent moiré patterning.) The examples shown here have been printed at a very low screen frequency so that the halftone patterning is visible to the naked eye. However, the rationale behind these traditional angles has to do with making the patterning of each color as unobtrusive to the eye as possible.

Cyan: 105 degrees

Magenta: 75 degrees

Yellow: 90 degrees

Composite CMYK image

Black: 45 degrees

Figure C–3

AM versus FM screening.
We used this desert scene from Hope, Arizona to show differences between two screening technologies. AM screening (digital halftoning; **left**) represents color and tone using variably sized dots spaced evenly on a grid. With FM screening (sometimes called stochastic screening; **below**), color and tone are represented by fixed-size or variable-size dots spaced at random intervals, thus eliminating patterning altogether. The FM screening in this image was generated with Icefields from Isis Imaging Corp.

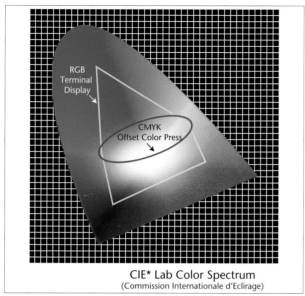

CIE* Lab Color Spectrum
(Commission Internationale d'Eclirage)

Graphic courtesy Tektronix Corp.

Figure C–4

CIE color space. *The perceptual CIE color space describes the entire range of colors that the human eye can detect. The CIE gamut forms the basis for color management systems (CMS) software because it is much larger than (and contains) both the additive RGB and the subtractive CMYK gamuts. This diagram (**left**) shows the relationships between the gamuts of each color space.*

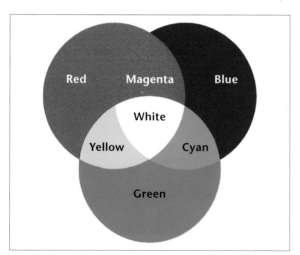

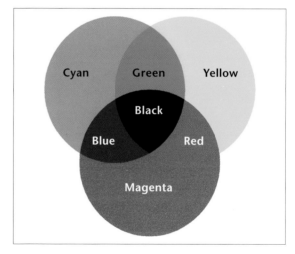

Figure C–5

RGB and CMY color models. *In the additive RGB color space that describes how digital devices reproduce color (**left**), combinations of red, green, and blue produce all available colors by adding light to light. Maximum intensities of red, green, and blue combine to produce white; two-color combinations produce the complementary colors (cyan, magenta, and yellow). In the subtractive CMY color space used by the printing industry (**right**), cyan, magenta, and yellow combine to generate all printable colors. Theoretically, maximum intensities of CMY should produce pure black. In practice, a muddy brown is produced due to imperfections in ink pigments and a deliberate imbalance toward cyan in the color separation process. Printers therefore use black as a fourth key (K) color to contour the depth of CMY gamuts.*

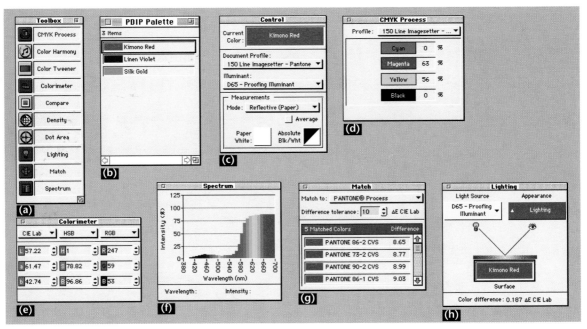

Figure C–6

Colortron controls. *Each of the Colortron's modular palettes has specific uses in a color management context.* **(a)** *The customizable Toolbox gives you immediate access to up to ten frequently-used modules.* **(b)** *User-definable color palettes let you name and save all the colors used in a project or publication.* **(c)** *The Control module stores information about the parameters under which each color in a palette is used or viewed.* **(d)** *The CMYK Process module displays exact CMYK equivalents based on an output color profile.* **(e)** *The Colorimeter module translates a measured color to its nearest equivalents in three user-specified color spaces.* **(f)** *The Spectrum module displays the current color's spectral wavelengths and intensities.* **(g)** *The Match module displays the closest PANTONE spot or process colors within a specified color difference range.* **(h)** *The Lighting module displays a color under a variety of real-world lighting conditions.*

© Emil Ihrig

Figure C–7

Contouring and the black channel. *When managed properly, the black channel adds depth to an image.* **Far left:** *This image, separated using only CMY inks, lacks definition in transitional areas.* **Right:** *The addition of a black plate (here, with a medium amount of black generation) makes color transitions appear crisper. Figure 6–1 shows how variations in the amount of black generation affect contouring throughout an image.*

Figure C-8

Black generation and neutral subjects.
Color images in which the chief subjects have neutral content (whites, grayscales, or metallics) benefit from higher amounts of black generation, which helps reduce the risk of color casts. The component channels for this example image, separated with a heavy amount of black, appear in Figure 6–2.

© Emil Ihrig

Courtesy MetaTools, Inc.

Figure C-9

GCR/UCA separation for low-key and full-range color images. The best candiates for GCR/UCA separations are low-key images and other images which, like this example, need to remain deeply colorful in all brightness ranges, including the shadow tones. Specifying UCA ensures that the CMY primaries replace some of the black in darker color ranges to ensure richer colors. Total ink coverage is higher with GCR/UCA than with GCR alone, so reserve UCA separations for images that will be printed on high-quality coated stocks. Figure 6–3 shows how black and the CMY primaries are distributed in a typical GCR/UCA separation.

© Emil Ihrig

Figure C-10

UCR for images with neutral shadow content. As a color separation technique, under color removal (UCR) tends to flatten color in darker tonal ranges, where larger amounts of black are substituted for the CMY primaries. UCR's preferred use is therefore for images where shadow content needs to stay neutral. UCR offers protection against color casts in such images and also reduces total ink coverage, making it a good tool for publications that will be printed on uncoated stocks. Figure 6–4 shows a typical distribution of inks in a UCR separation.

© Emil Ihrig

© Emil Ihrig

Figure C–11

Converting color to black and white. *Color images can exhibit up to three different types of contrast—luminosity, hue, and purity—but black-and-white images can have only one type, luminosity. This explains why many color images look murky and lack contouring when converted to grayscale without additional processing. The two images shown here convert quite differently to black and white (see Figure 6–6).* **Left**: *This example features strong light-to-dark contrast and so converts to grayscale successfully.* **Right**: *This image, on the other hand, chiefly contains contrast in hue and luminosity, both of which are lost in making the transition to grayscale. Channel-by-channel adjustments to the image perk up its contrast and contouring sufficiently to generate an acceptable black-and-white version (Figure 6–8) .*

© Emil Ihrig

Figure C–12

Deriving a black-and-white conversion from a single RGB channel. When a composite color original does not contain sufficient luminosity contrast to produce a successful grayscale conversion, it is sometimes possible to generate a good black-and-white version by blending two of the color channels. The subject matter can provide clues about which channels contain the best luminosity contrast for blending purposes.
Above: *This color image emphasizes two different subjects—skin tones, which are basically red, and foliage, which is predominantly green—indicating that the red and green RGB channels would make the best candidates for conversion. Neither channel is perfect for both subjects at once; the red channel (**right, top**) contains the optimum contrast, but the green channel (**right, bottom**) contains a broader tonal range and better detail. Blending the two as shown in Figure 6–7 does justice to both subjects and to luminosity contrast, too.*

© Emil Ihrig

Figure C–13

Process-color multitones. Whether or not you work with Adobe Photoshop, you can use CMYK inks to generate single-color tints (multitones) with the look of traditional duotones. Multitones emphasize the tint color differently depending on the brightness ranges in which you allow the color to predominate. Here, we present two multitones that use all four process colors to simulate a cyan tint. **Left:** The tint color dominates the image because the colors other than black are strong in the midtones and highlights, where the eye perceives color most readily. **Right:** With the colors other than black now appearing nowhere except in small amounts in the midtones, the image has become essentially a monochrome, with details accentuated by a hint of color. Figure 6–10 shows how color is distributed in each of the CMYK channels for both cases.

© Emil Ihrig

Figure C–14

One image, many outcomes. The same image used for different purposes emphasizes color, contrast, and detail differently in each case. **Left:** This version, which downplays reds and saturates the yellows of the hair, would be appropriate for use in collateral materials published by a hair coloring or wig manufacturer. **Right:** This alternative version, which emphasizes the colors of the makeup, might well have been prepared for a cosmetics advertisement.

© Emil Ihrig

Figure C–15

Casts in whites and neutrals. The human eye is especially sensitive to color casts in subjects that should print as white or neutral. When such a cast is present, as in the case of the red-casted imitation snow in a display case (***above***), it most likely affects other tonal ranges as well. The entire image should be adjusted to neutralize the unwanted color shift (***below***). Figure 8–1 shows the curve adjustments made to the magenta and yellow channels to eliminate the cast.

© Emil Ihrig

Figure C–16

Casts in memory colors. *The eye is quick to detect color casts in universally recognizable memory colors, such as the skin tones featured in this shady original (**above**). Neutralizing the all-too-blue cast requires shifting selected color ranges away from blues and cyans and toward reds and yellows, resulting in more natural-looking skin tones (**below**). Figure 8–3 shows how Photoshop's Selective Colors command helped to effect these color shifts.*

© Emil Ihrig

Figure C–17

Neutralizing cross-curve casts. Some photographically processed images exhibit one color cast in the highlights and a complementary-color cast in the midtones or shadows (**top**). In these cases, simply making global curve adjustments doesn't solve the problem because, in the process of removing one offending cast, the subjects in other tonal ranges can shift drastically toward the complementary cast. In our example (**center**), using curves to eliminate excessive green from the highlight and quartertone subjects (pavement, posts, and vehicles) causes the colors of the midtone subjects (the sky and the triangular marquees) to become weighted heavily toward magenta. To correct both casts without introducing color distortions, it is often necessary to clean up local selections separately after eliminating the highlight cast. In our example (**bottom**), we used curves to completely neutralize the green cast in the highlights and quartertones and then followed up with Photoshop's Select Color and Selective Color commands to correct the resulting distorted colors of the marquee and sky. Figure 8–2 shows the main steps used to carry out this strategy.

Figure C–18

*Enhancing color, saturation, and detail. The original image (**immediate right**), though acceptable in quality, would benefit from deeper reds in the flag, brighter lighting overall, and heightened grain in the wood. After applying the curves shown in Figure 8–4, the adjusted image (**far right**) appears crisper, with improved contrast, more vivid detail, and truer, more intense colors.*

© Emil Ihrig

Figure C–19

*Increasing saturation. When vivifying colors is the primary goal, adjustments to hue, saturation, and lightness often work more efficiently (and with less risk of introducing color casts) than curve-based manipulations. **Top right:** The white wicker chair in this garden scene is brilliant enough, but the magenta chair pad looks dull and the grass less than lush. **Below:** Saturation and lightness changes to greens and magentas through the use of Photoshop's Hue/Saturation controls affect colors selectively. **Below right:** The color in the resulting image has considerably more snap.*

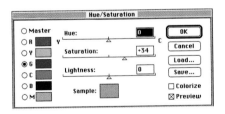

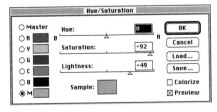

© Emil Ihrig

© Emil Ihrig

Figure C–20

Improving color depth. An image with too much brilliance and too little tonal depth (**left**) lacks contrast in the primary component colors and has a black channel that's too light to provide good detail. The version with improved depth (**right**) was produced by generating a second set of separations with a heavier black channel, blending the new black channel with the more richly detailed yellow channel, and substituting the manufactured black channel for the original. Figure 8–5 compares the original and enhanced channels and shows the techniques used to achieve the final result.

© Emil Ihrig

Figure C-21

Cleansing murky colors. *These Tiffany lamps (**left**) suffer from a general muddiness that obstructs their otherwise colorful content. The more brilliant colors in the enhanced version (**right**) result from creating duplicate separations with different settings, blending old and new versions of the flat and heavy yellow channel, eliminating lighter values of black from the duplicate black channel, and engineering greater contrast into the black. Figure 8–6 shows the key steps involved in the enhancement process.*

Figure C–22

Effective single-channel sharpening in LAB mode.
*Converting an RGB or CMYK image to LAB color, sharpening just the Luminance channel in LAB mode, and then (re)converting the image to CMYK with specific color separation settings can be an effective sharpening technique. The original version of this outdoor scene (**left**) is milky, but applying unsharp masking to just the Luminance channel results in a definitely sharper version with crisper contouring (**right**). Figure 10–4 shows the Luminance channel sharpening process.*

© Emil Ihrig

forward 20 percent above 50 percent). This second, absolute method is the one used by most image-editing and color separations programs. Find out the background of the person who gives you the information and verify how he or she is measuring dot gain so you can ensure that your software and your real-world sources are speaking the same language.

There's a common misconception about setting dot gain in Photoshop. Many users assume that specifying a certain amount of dot gain automatically corrects the color values of the image to compensate for the expected gain. In reality, the dot gain percentage only causes the onscreen image to appear darker so that you can compensate visually using tone curves; your entry has no impact on the conversion of color values during the color separation process. See Chapter 7 for examples of how to make curve-based adjustments to compensate for anticipated dot gain.

After you've gathered all the necessary information to ensure a correct color separation and have actually converted the image, it's time to forge forward with tonal and color adjustments. Before you do, though, take a look at the "Gray Balance: Neutral Is Not Equal" sidebar to familiarize yourself with what to look for when examining CMYK values.

From Color to Black and White

The moguls of the digital prepress industry would have you believe that we're unanimously rushing out to print four-color documents like lemmings to the sea. We're not. For one thing, not all publishers have the budget to print in process color. For another, black-and-white images can look extremely elegant. Witness the rash of black-and-white advertisements in upscale consumer magazines in recent years, or the many printed examples of monochromatic color used sparingly against a grayscale background. Finally, those of you in advertising know how important it is to preserve two versions of an image for different markets: one in color, the other in grayscale.

So, black and white is here to stay. But with the proliferation of color capabilities among even the most modest digital cameras and desktop scanners, receiving source images already digitized and in color is becoming an increasingly common occurrence. You're left with the task of deriving a high-quality black-and-white image from an RGB or CMYK original that might range from the stellar to the mediocre. And there's the rub. How can you make the transition from color to black and white without sacrificing essential detail, contrast, and crispness? It's not a five-second cinch, but the principles are straightforward. Best of all, the tools to do it digitally are at your command.

Why Black and White Falls Flat

Figure C–11 in the Color Gallery and Figure 6–6 show examples of two color images converted to black and white with no preliminary processing. The first image translates beautifully with contrast and detail intact, while the second comes out murky and flat. Yet both color originals are equal in quality. What happened?

The disappointing appearance of the second image stems from the fact that color can embody as many as three different types of contrast, whereas black and white can manifest only one.

- *Luminosity*, or contrast in brightness levels, is the only type of contrast that black-and-white and color images have in common. If a color image is rich in light-to-dark contrasts, it will translate well into black and white with little or no apparent loss in quality.

Figure 6–6   © Emil Ihrig

*The degree of inherent luminosity contrast in a color image determines how successfully it converts to grayscale without additional adjustments. **Left:** the color original of this pelican photo (see Figure C–11) contains ample light-to-dark contrast, so the grayscale version (derived from the blue channel in RGB mode) looks crisp and detailed. **Right:** this flat grayscale results from a color original that features high contrast in hues and purity, but low contrast in terms of brightness levels. Figure 6–8 shows how we engineered enough light-to-dark contrast into the color original to generate an acceptable grayscale conversion.*

- Contrast in *hue* applies to color images only. For example, magenta and green are complementary colors, and so our eyes perceive the green lotus leaves against the purplish background of Figure C–1 as being high in contrast. But when we convert to black and white, the hues are lost; detail in the leaves no longer stands out.

- We also perceive differences in the *purity* of adjacent colors as contrast. In the rightmost image in Figure 6–6, for example, both the nymph's head and the lotus leaves behind it are green, but the green of the lotus is purer and more saturated; the nymph's head contains a greater admixture of other colors, so we perceive con-

trast between the two subjects. But when we translate these colors to black and white, both subjects have similar levels of brightness. Result: sparkle and detail seem to disappear.

To summarize: some color images naturally translate well to black and white, while others don't. The situation isn't hopeless, though. When confronted with less-than-perfect color-to-black-and-white candidates, one or more of these remedies is guaranteed to help you salvage image quality:

- Hone your evaluation skills to determine what kinds of contrast exist in the color version;

- Engineer some light-to-dark contrast into the color original before converting to grayscale; or

- Become comfortable working with channels so you can pluck data from the channel(s) that contain the greatest luminosity contrast.

Evaluating Color for Contrast

Learning to evaluate color images with a critical eye will help you determine what kinds of contrast exist in them (there may be more than one). Armed with that information, you can then decide what you need to do to optimize the contrast in luminosity if necessary.

Experts disagree over whether you should perform contrast-enhancing adjustments in RGB or in CMYK. Since excellent results can be obtained either way, it makes sense to work in whatever color space the image is digitized in—RGB for desktop-scanned and digital camera captures, and CMYK for drum-scanned originals. We'll present both approaches and let you take your pick.

Evaluating in and Converting from RGB

Here's an approach to preparing a color image for conversion to black and white without ever leaving the RGB color space.

1. Begin by viewing the RGB channels individually to see which one offers the best contrast potential. Let the subject matter serve as your guide. Portraits, fashion photos, and other images that emphasize skin tones convert best to grayscale if you single out the red channel and darken it slightly. Nature scenes that feature plants often convert best from the green channel, while seashore scenes may convert well from the blue channel.

2. If no single channel seems promising enough to base a grayscale version on it, consider blending two of the RGB channels (see Figure 6–7 and Figure C–12 in the Color Gallery). Experienced photographers who are accustomed to using lens-based filters will adapt to this technique easily.

Evaluating in CMYK

Many imaging professionals prefer to engineer the perfect black and white from a CMYK color version, maintaining that the larger number of channels gives greater leverage in making adjustments. Follow these steps to evaluate a CMYK image for its best grayscale potential:

1. If the image is in RGB color, start by converting it to CMYK. Make certain, of course, that you've set up color separation parameters correctly first.

Red channel

Green channel

Blended channel (red and green)

© Emil Ihrig

Figure 6–7

The color original in Figure C–12 emphasizes two different subjects—skin tones and foliage—indicating that the red and green channels would make the best candidates for conversion. Neither channel is perfect—the red channel contains the optimum contrast, but the green channel contains a broader tonal range and better detail—so blending the two yields the best black-and-white conversion.

2. Display a histogram of the composite image. If the colors are concentrated in one tonal area, there will be very little light-to-dark contrast in the image. If colors are spread throughout the tonal spectrum, the prognosis is somewhat better. The best case is a histogram that shows both a broad range of tones *and* peaks and valleys in the distribution of colors, rather than a single bell curve.

3. Review each CMYK channel and its histogram individually to determine which channels show acceptable levels of luminosity contrast and which ones need beefing up. Taking the color original in Figure C–11 as an example, we found that contrast in the important subject matter was weakest in the magenta and black channels—that's logical if you recall that the magenta channel controls green, while the black channel provides contouring for the entire image. Figure 6–8 shows the original magenta and black channels, the curves used to intensify contrast, the final magenta and black channels, and the "before and after" conversions to black and white.

4. If a histogram reveals that you'll need to increase light-to-dark contrast in order to achieve a successful conversion, decide which subjects are the most important ones to emphasize. These are the subjects into which you'll need to introduce higher contrast levels to bring out latent detail. In the example in Figure 6–8, for instance, it's important to heighten apparent contrast between the lotus leaves and the nymph's head, between the lotus leaves and the background, and within the features of the nymph's head itself.

5. Using an eyedropper tool, survey the important subject areas and the subjects that you want to contrast them with. Get a feel for the variations in grayscale percentages within these subject areas and for the types of color contrast that predominate—hue, purity, or both. Your contrast-enhancement strategy will differ for each type.

Retaining the Color in Gray

Determining where you need to strengthen light-to-dark contrast is the hard part; actually doing the strengthening is the easy part, despite the fact that you're working in CMYK or RGB. Correcting color for conversion to black and white has some advantages over correcting color for color output. You don't have to worry about how strange the colors start looking in the process, and you don't need to concern yourself about realism or color casts. In other respects, the correction techniques are similar, as you'll see when you get to Chapter 8. The principles are easy to grasp:

- To enhance detail *within* a given brightness range, flatten the curve slightly in those areas and steepen it in the areas lighter and darker than that brightness range.

- To introduce contrast *between* adjacent colors, steepen the curve in the range that contains those colors.

- When the predominant type of contrast in a color image is contrast between hues, concentrate your efforts in the channels that control those printed colors. Think in terms of both primary colors (cyan, magenta, and yellow) and complementary colors: cyan controls red, yellow controls blue, and magenta controls green. Work on combinations of channels when dealing with other colors, such as orange or purple.

- When the predominant type of contrast is one of color purity, concentrate your efforts in the channels that control the components of the less-pure colors.

Figure 6–8

© Emil Ihrig

Examination of the component channels in the color original in Figure C–11 shows that the luminosity contrast is weakest in the magenta and black channels. Intensifying contrast in the important subject areas of the magenta [(a), (b), and (c)] and black [(d), (e), and (f)] channels makes the difference between a washed-out black-and-white conversion (g) and one that shows a more acceptable balance of contrast and detail (h).

You usually can work most efficiently by zeroing in on problems in specific color channels, rather than taking the sledgehammer approach of trying to adjust the composite image in one fell swoop. In the color original from which the weak black-and-white conversion in Figure 6–6 was derived, for example, the predominant types of contrast are hue and purity. The magenta and black channels evidence the weakest contrast levels—especially in the 30 to 50 and 70 to 90 percent ranges of the magenta channel and in the 15 to 55 percent range of the black channel. Our strategy (illustrated in Figure 6–8) is therefore to steepen the magenta and black curves in those ranges. The strange colors that result when you make these types of adjustments usually don't look like anything you'd want to commit to print in the name of realism! But you shouldn't care about these matters when the goal is to obtain an acceptable black-and-white image.

Alternative Contrast-Boosting Strategies

The examples given in the foregoing section represent just a smattering of techniques to boost luminosity contrast in a color image before converting it to black and white. There are plenty of other approaches you could take. For instance:

- Blend the RGB or CMYK plate that has the strongest inherent contrast in the important subject matter with the plate that has the weakest. Then substitute the new channel for the one that was formerly weak. This is an advanced technique that takes practice in determining the best blend percentages and the most important brightness ranges to manipulate.

- Boost contrast in the black channel for CMYK images. Use an S-shaped curve in the brightness ranges that require the most intense enhancements to contrast and detail.

Tip: Obtaining good grayscales from color is a prerequisite for generating decent duotones from a color original.

Scanning Color for Black-and-White Output

On occasion, you may need to scan a color original that you know will be output to black and white. Should you scan in color or grayscale? We vote for color. Color originals have the potential of yielding much better black-and-white results than grayscale originals can. This is because nonprofessional photographers tend to view color as color, even when their film is black and white. Equally important, color film has seen more technological improvements in recent years than black-and-white emulsions have. Whereas color films of the past were relatively thick, leading to softer images and reduced definition, today's color films approach the thinness of black-and-white films. Conclusion: it's to your advantage to shoot and scan all images in color and then create an aesthetically inspired black-and-white conversion in your image-editing package. Starting with color gives you the greatest amount of control.

Four-Color Grays

If a publication contains both color and black-and-white images (a common phenomenon among magazines, newsletters, and newspapers), printing the grayscale images as four-color black and whites makes sense aesthetically as well as economically—four-color grays look richer and higher in contrast than grays printed from the black plate alone. The main risk with printing black and white in CMYK is that the vagaries of presswork might introduce unwanted color casts (see Chapter 8). You can help prevent these when you convert the grayscale image to CMYK. Simply adjust your color separation parameters to generate a medium to heavy black, rather than the light black you would use with most CMYK images printed in color. Having the extra weight of black helps maintain the neutrality of your grays.

Creating Multitones

A *multitone* is essentially any black-and-white image printed with two or more inks to create the appearance of a solid color tint. Multitones, examples of which are shown in Figure C–13 in the Color Gallery, are a popular and effective design tool. They add depth and apparent detail to monochrome images. They heighten the sense of color in the pages of publications that can afford only two- or three-color printing. They also create special visual accents in four-color publications or publications that have a fifth, custom color ink at their disposal.

Tip: Generating multitones requires that you start with a grayscale image. If the original for the grayscale image is in color, remember to increase light-to-dark contrast as outlined in the earlier parts of this chapter before converting to black and white.

You can achieve a tinted look for a monochrome image using one of two basic methods: the Photoshop duotone method or the process multitone method.

The Photoshop Duotone Method

If you'll be printing with spot colors only, or with custom ink colors in addition to CMYK, you can use Adobe Photoshop's standard presets for *duotones* (two-tone images printed using black and one spot or custom color ink), *tritones* (tints created using three different inks), and *quadtones* (tints created with four ink colors). Photoshop offers a well-documented, flexible method for creating multitones that allows a certain amount of control over determining the brightness levels in which you want the additional (tint) colors to predominate (Figure 6–9).

The "pure" Photoshop method has a few potential disadvantages, depending on your level of comfort in editing tone curves and other factors.

- Once you create a duotone, there's no way to view channels for the various ink colors separately. Photoshop creates a single duotone channel for the file. (This is no problem for output, though; the major page layout packages separate a duotone file into its component CMYK separations automatically.)

- If you want to edit tone curves manually, you're limited to manipulating 10 percent increments in the proprietary duotone channel. You can't edit tone curves for the component colors unless you first convert the image to CMYK (see the "Four-Color Multitones" section immediately following).

- There's no way for you to adjust the amount of black generated during the separation and output process unless you first convert the image to CMYK.

- Photoshop's proprietary format for multitones requires saving the file in EPS, so take extra care with file format options so that you don't lock in halftone screen or other settings with the file unintentionally.

Four-Color Multitones

It's entirely possible to create the look of a single tint color using the standard CMYK inks. Read on if you want maximum control over the multitones you generate with Photoshop, or

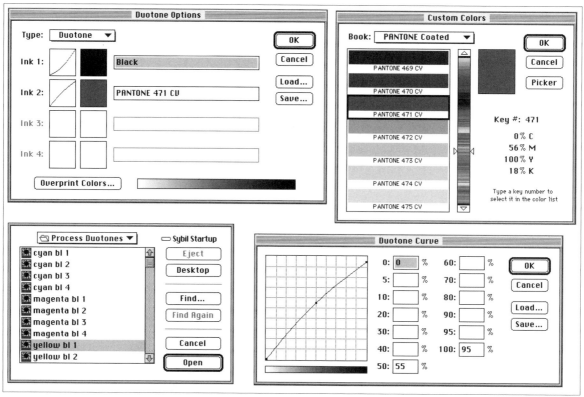

Figure 6–9

Photoshop's Duotone Options dialog box lets you choose one or more tint colors based on industry-standard spot or process color pickers. Many built-in presets make it easy to alter the balance between black and additional colors in ways that generate a smooth, even tint. You can also edit the tone curves for the presets in 10 percent increments.

if you use some other image-editing program instead and want to create "generic" tints.

If you want to create process-color multitones *and* you use Photoshop, here's the basic procedure to follow:

1. Generate a multitone using the standard Photoshop method. If you want a tint color that simulates something more complex than cyan, magenta, or yellow, use one of the process color finders (Trumatch or Focoltone, for example).

2. Set Black Generation to Medium or Heavy in the Separation Setup dialog box (assuming you'll be using GCR instead of

UCR). Having extra black guards against color casts due to sloppy presswork (something the proprietary Photoshop duotone format doesn't compensate for).

3. Convert the image from Duotone to CMYK. Figure 6–10 shows the separations for the process multitone image pictured in Figure C–13.

Once you're back in the realm of CMYK, you can refine the tone curves of individual channels slightly, just as you would when performing normal color correction (see Chapter 8). This gives you an advantage when your goal is to bring out specific details.

Caution: *Tweak CMYK curves for multitones with care to avoid corrupting the single-color look. Make only minor adjustments at a time and preview the CMYK result at each step.*

If you work with a program other than Photoshop, you can create generic CMYK tints using a do-it-yourself method. Here's an exam-

ple of how to create a simple cyan, magenta, or yellow pseudo-duotone:

1. Start with a relatively high-contrast, black-and-white image. Be sure to heighten luminosity contrast in color originals that you convert to grayscale.

2. Create a duplicate of the grayscale image and check the color separation parameters

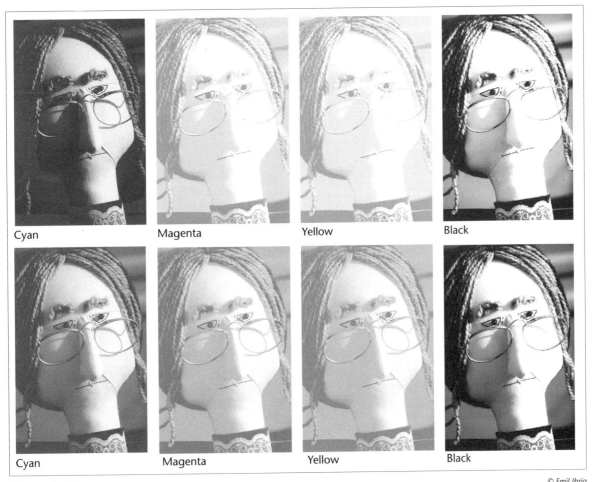

Cyan   Magenta   Yellow   Black

Cyan   Magenta   Yellow   Black

© Emil Ihrig

Figure 6–10
*The CMYK separations for two of the standard Photoshop Cyan/Black duotone presets shown in Figure C–13 make it easy to see how each preset redistributes process color inks differently to alter the relative emphasis between black and the tint color—in this case, one in which cyan predominates. **Top:** separations for the most saturated color version of the tint. **Bottom:** separations for the process duotone in which black most strongly dominates the tint color.*

to ensure that you have heavy black generation selected. Then convert the duplicate to CMYK, select all, and delete the contents of the image so that you're left with a blank CMYK starter.

3. Select the entire black-and-white image and copy it into the black channel of the blank CMYK image.

4. Select the entire grayscale image once more and copy it into the channel that corresponds to the tint you want to achieve.

5. Edit the curve for each channel in a way that reflects the color intensity and distribution you want to achieve. Your curves for the black channel will have a very different shape from the curve for the color channel.

If you want to use a PANTONE or other spot color instead of cyan, magenta, or yellow, no problem. Just tell your print vendor to substitute the spot color ink for the process color ink. (That's assuming you're using tinted images throughout the document instead of mixing process images and tints in the same set of separations.) If, on the other hand, you want to use a complex CMYK color rather than a spot color for your tint, things get a little more hairy. You'll need to become extremely proficient at curve-based correction in order to determine how to shape a single, smooth tint using four different variables.

Multitone Design Guidelines

Multitones aren't foolproof. There are some basic guidelines you can follow to ensure an elegant, eye-pleasing look for your tints.

- Start with a high-contrast, relatively detailed black-and-white original. Review the "From Color to Black and White" section of this chapter for assistance on how to wrest the best balance between contrast and detail from a converted color image.

- Choose subdued colors over loud ones. Overly brilliant colors tend to wash out detail in the midtone and lighter areas, leading to a milky look.

- Choose darker colors when your primary aim is to enhance detail in the darker tones and lighter colors when your goal is to introduce the feel of more color into a monochrome image.

- When using a dark color for the tint, create a concave curve in the midtones for that color channel (see Chapter 7) to prevent heaviness in the details of medium brightness.

- When using a light color for the tint, create a convex curve in the midtones for its color channel so that lighter details aren't overwhelmed by the black.

- When using a medium-bright color, vary the midtones for its channel only slightly.

- Shape the curve for each channel according to the effects you want to achieve. If you want to introduce just a hint of color, for example, pull the tint color back strongly in the highlights and midtones and leave the darker tones entirely black. For a saturated-color look, allow the tint color to pervade the entire light-to-dark spectrum and increase its amount in the light-to-medium bright areas.

Converting images from one color mode to another is often the foundation for a great print job. We hope you've discovered in this chapter that converting images can be more than a perfectionist's playground—it can be challenging and fun as well.

Tonal Correction for Output

Many print communications professionals have the mistaken impression that as long as their scanner, monitor, and final output device are calibrated to one another, no further image correction or enhancement procedures are necessary. Given the current industry obsession with color management, this notion is understandable, but it's far removed from reality. While color management is an important first step in preparing an image for print, it's hardly a panacea. The kaleidoscopic interplay between input source, image content, document goals, press type, and paper stock means that every image demands a unique approach to adjusting and improving tone and color.

Optimizing an image for print actually involves many different techniques, which often get lumped together under the common rubric of *image correction*, *image processing*, or *image enhancement*. We'll outline some general principles of image correction in the first part of this chapter. Then, we'll discuss one of the most essential steps in image processing, *tonal correction*—adjusting brightness levels at the extremes and in the middle of the tonal range specifically to compensate for the limitations of the printing process. Chapter 8 picks up where this chapter leaves off to discuss enhancements that relate strictly to color, and Chapter 10 covers sharpening and other special types of adjustments.

Image Correction Principles

Before we plunge into the hands-on how-tos, we think it's important to debunk some popular myths. Lest you be tempted to view the processes of correction and enhancement as a welter of hard and fast rules and regulations, keep the following points in mind.

What's the Goal? Or, Why Your Vacation Photos Don't Live Up to Your Memories

The term *correction* implies that an image falls short of meeting a standard and requires adjustment to make it measure up. The term *enhancement*, on the other hand, suggests that you're improving image quality in a way that exceeds the standard. Question is, what *is* the standard? What's the goal of correction and enhancement? All too often, we assume that we should slavishly match an undigitized original, when in fact our true aim should be to draw out the best potential of the subject matter in a way that heightens its intended message. These two goals lead in separate directions; let's explore why.

The Eyes Have It

The human eye has an amazing capacity to see what it wants to see—to compensate for color casts and changes to lighting in the immediate environment. The camera is much more objective. When that gorgeous ocean sunset scene you photographed on your summer vacation comes back from the developer, the water doesn't seem as deeply blue nor the sky as brilliantly orange as you remember it. In fact, the whole doggone scene is probably too

dark to distinguish detail. But before you begin cursing the film or the development process, consider that the camera may have been faithful to reality—it's just that your eyes adjusted to the dim lighting and were therefore able to perceive the deeply saturated colors that the camera could not.

This example illustrates that in many cases, the human eye is a more reliable standard to follow than a camera. That's especially true today; many stock photos, for example, now originate from diverse sources of variable quality, and Photo CD images inevitably look a little too soft. The human eye is also the standard in advertising, in product catalogs, and in other applications where images are used for persuasion purposes. Even scientific and medical images sometimes require beefing up colors in order to present "reality" more forcefully.

The printing process places several obstacles in the way of obtaining perfect reproduction as the eye would see it. In addition to correcting an image *to* a standard of vivid, credible colors, crisp detail, and balanced contrast, it's necessary to correct *for* the vagaries of paper stock, press type, and dot gain. The many details to which you need to attend when carrying out color separation and image correction processes owe their existence to these factors.

More Than One Path to the Same Destination

There's no single "right" way to adjust a given image. The uses to which you will put the image determines the overall approach. The eye of the beholder is another variable; any two imaging professionals are likely to come up with two different final versions because of the subjective decisions they must make. Take a look at Figure C–14 in the Color Gallery for an example of how divergent goals can dictate a variety of outcomes for the same image.

Garbage In, Gems Out

You're probably familiar with the industry dictum that nothing can be done to salvage a source image that's less than sterling to start with. If that were true, you'd have to consign a majority of today's scanned, captured, and stock images to the flames. More and more images are being created by untrained photgraphers and digitized with lower-end equipment rather than with dedicated drum scanners, but that doesn't mean you have to give up your aspirations to excellence. The fact is, most print media simply can't reproduce the full range of tones in the high-end scans anyway; the tonal range always needs to be compressed, which requires further adjustments to the image to ensure that the printed version still looks crisp and saturated.

Our position is that if you have a firm grasp of basic correction techniques, you can make even mediocre scans, digital captures, and Photo CD images sing in print. So give the GIGO acronym a new meaning—Garbage In, Gems Out—not Garbage In, Garbage Out.

Correct in the Optimum Color Space

If an image is in color and your image-editing package permits, tonal and color correction ideally should take place in the CMYK color space. Consider these advantages:

- It's the native color space for the printing process.
- CMYK has a more limited gamut than RGB (see Chapter 4), and bright colors, deep blues, and saturated greens are difficult to achieve. Seeing how colors shift from RGB to the duller CMYK mode lets you more accurately determine the extent to which image colors will need altering to reproduce the way you want them to.

- Having four image channels to work with instead of three gives you more options and greater leverage for making adjustments when you reach the color correction phase.

That said, keep in mind that the CMYK color space is not one to enter into lightly. Whenever you shift from RGB or any other mode into CMYK, you are creating a digital color separation, and unless you set up color separation parameters correctly in advance, you may introduce incorrect ink limits or imbalances between the various color plates that will be difficult to rectify either digitally or on press. Clear, timely communication with your print and/or prepress vendor regarding essential press parameters is important (see Chapter 6 for guidelines). It's not necessarily a liability if you don't have the correct color separation information early in the production process; many programs let you preview a CMYK version of an image as you work in RGB mode. That won't help you with tonal correction, but it will allow you to perform some color-related adjustments until you've gathered all the necessary press setup information.

Tip: *There are times when other color spaces can help you perform adjustment acrobatics more efficiently than CMYK can. Working in Photoshop's LAB color mode, for example, you can improve the crispness and detail of colors in Photo CD and desktop-scanned images, which tend toward a slight fuzziness (see Chapter 10).*

Correction by the Numbers

Whether or not your system is calibrated, use numerical values, not the appearance of an image on the monitor, as the final arbiter for all tonal and color adjustment decisions. Bright light sources such as monitors skew our perception of relative brightness levels, particularly in the lightest areas of an image. Figure 7–1

Figure 7–1   © Emil Ihrig

*The bright light source in a computer monitor deceives the eye about color values in lighter areas of an image. To avoid washed-out highlights (**top**) and preserve detail in the lightest areas (**bottom**), place your faith in numerical values rather than in the eye alone.*

illustrates a common error to which imaging professionals who rely solely on their eyes fall prey: a light subject, such as the delicate shading in the lace garments of the dancers, may look perfectly adjusted on the monitor but print with the very lightest details washed out to white (or to the color of the paper stock). You can easily avoid such errors by using an eyedropper or onscreen densitometer tool to spot-check values, and by setting highlight and shadow values numerically.

Make Corrections Globally

When you see colors that you know are wrong—green fluorescent lights in a night scene, for example—the sophistication of today's selection and masking tools makes it tempting to select just the offending colors and apply corrections to limited areas. Think again. Tonal and color corrections tend to be more effective when you apply them globally than when you tinker with selected areas alone. That's because the color shifts known as *color casts* usually pervade an entire image, even when you perceive them only in important subject areas or specific color ranges. Once again, we have the ever-adaptable human eye to thank for this phenomenon of misperception!

Of course, there are occasions when you need to enhance specific subjects in an image (say, a clothing article in a catalog photo), and masking techniques can be lifesavers for such instances. But use them with discretion and only *after* making adjustments to the image as a whole.

Use Curves to Make Most Adjustments

Think of yourself as a doctor and an uncorrected image as your patient. Any doctor worth his or her salt needs both a correct diagnosis and correct treatment procedures to make the patient well. As your primary diagnostic tools, use a histogram to determine tonal distribution in the composite image and in individual channels, and an eyedropper tool to verify the subject areas in which critical tonal ranges fall. But when it's time to apply treatment, the tone curves that you shape for each channel are usually the most effective medicine.

Tip: *Changes to tone curves are relative to the original diagonal line. Steepening a curve compresses brightness levels in the affected tonal range, adding contrast and making detail "pop" there. Flattening a curve expands brightness levels in the affected tonal range, decreasing contrast there but making available detail more visible (though not sharper).*

Sound Image Correction Practices

Image correction and enhancement is an organic process involving many interrelated tasks, but you can work more efficiently if you complete them in a specific order. Here's a sequence that works well for most images:

- Size the image to the correct output size and resolution.
- Sharpen the image to compensate for softness introduced by scanning (input) and printing (output) procedures.
- Identify the tonal character of the image.
- Convert the image (if it's in color) to CMYK, using the correct color separation parameters for your project (see Chapter 6).
- Determine which tonal ranges in the image are the most and least important to enhance based on subject matter.
- Define the highlight values based on printer specifications, taking the tonal character and content of the image into account.
- Define the shadow values based on printer specifications, again taking the tonal character and content of the image into account.

- Adjust the midtones to compensate for anticipated dot gain. If you use Photoshop, you can accomplish this task visually after you've nailed down the correct Printing Ink Setup parameters. You can compensate for dot gain numerically using any program that offers curve-based adjustments.
- Re-examine the highlights and look for neutral colors and memory colors in the image (see Chapter 8). Determine numerically whether these contain any unwanted color casts. If so, adjust them by working in individual channels.
- Examine each color channel for potential contrast and detail problems based on subject matter and adjust the image accordingly.
- Make sure that the image is at the correct resolution for optimum output.

You'll find detailed coverage of each of these steps in Chapters 6 through 10 as well as in the current chapter.

Tip: *Be sure to undertake most of these steps only after consulting with and receiving the blessing of your print vendor!*

Tonal Range Basics

Graphic arts print reproduction professionals distinguish among seven different segments of the tonal range, shown in Figure 7–2. These distinctions are useful for defining the distribution of color or grayscale values in an image and for helping to determine how best to adjust each image. You'll encounter these terms frequently throughout this chapter.

- The *white point* is any area of an image that should *print* as pure white with no visible detail, even if that area is some other color when you first begin the image correction process. Not all images contain white subjects, so don't assume that you must automatically set a white point for every image you work on. The white point for any project is closely allied to the highlight value, described next.

- *Highlights* are the lightest areas of an image that still contain detail. In "printerspeak," the recommended highlight value is synonymous with the smallest dot percentage that the press can hold. Details in CMYK values that fall below the printer-recommended highlight value blow out to white (or the color of the paper). Typically, highlight values range from about 2 to about 10 percent depending on the press and paper characteristics for a given project.

- *Quartertones* are the values ranging from about 18 to about 35 percent, centered on 25 percent.

- *Midtones* are the values of medium brightness in an image, ranging from about 35 to about 65 percent and centered at 50 percent.

- *Three-quartertones* represent color or grayscales from about 65 to about 80 percent and are centered on the 75 percent point.

- *Shadows* are the darkest values in an image that still contain detail—the largest, darkest dot that the press can hold. Details in CMYK values that are higher than the printer-recommended shadow value plug up and print as solid black. As with highlights, the recommended shadow value for a given project depends on the com-

Figure 7–2

*The tonal range of any image can be broken down into seven segments (see photo): white point (**a**), highlights (**b**), quartertones (**c**), midtones (**d**), three-quartertones (**e**), shadows (**f**), and black point (**g**). Placing control points on a tone curve (**right**) limits the effects of adjustments to specific tonal ranges. (Control points in this example progress from white at the lower-left corner to black at the upper-right corner.)*

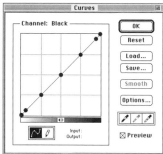

© Emil Ihrig

bination of press and paper stock to be used. Maximum shadow values range from about 75 percent for highly absorbent newsprint printed on a newspaper press up to about 98 percent for top-quality coated stocks printed on a sheet-fed press.

- The *black point* is any area of an image that should print as solid black—in other words, any area that's darker than the shadow value. You don't need to set a black point for a specific image unless that image actually contains subject matter that should print as black.

Identifying Tonal Character

Most images don't make use of the entire tonal range. Some images are extremely light, others extremely dark, and still others are heavily oriented toward the midtones. The part of the tonal range that predominates in the subject areas of greatest interest defines the *tonal character* or *key* of an image. Tonal character, in turn, determines some of the major adjustments you need to make to ensure that the important subjects in the image print with good contrast and detail and without excessive dot gain.

Print reproduction professionals define the tonal character of images according to one of three types. Figure 7–3 shows examples of each type of image, a typical histogram for each type, and typical curve adjustments to prepare each type for printing. The exact shapes of the curves you create will vary slightly from these examples, since you should always match curve shape to the specific tonal ranges occupied by the important subjects in an image.

- *High-key* images contain the most important details in the highlights and quartertones. The important subjects in a photograph of a polar bear in the snow at midday, for example, would be in bright, near-white areas such as the bear's fur. These lighter tones are sometimes called *diffuse highlights*. Midtone and shadow areas of high-key images contain relatively little detail of interest. To accentuate

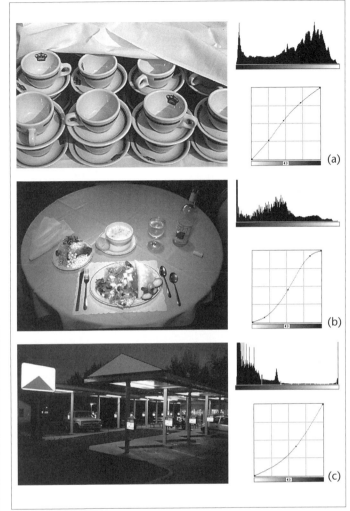

Figure 7–3

© Emil Ihrig

*The tonal character of an image determines which details you should emphasize for print reproduction and how best to optimize them. **(a)** High-key images show a preponderance of color or grayscale values at the right side of their histograms, indicating emphasis in the lighter tones. High-key images typically benefit from a curve adjustment that darkens the midtones and three-quartertones slightly. **(b)** Midtone or balanced images have histograms that are shaped like a bell curve or that show a preponderance of values in tones of medium brightness. To optimize midtone detail and create contrast with less important tonal areas, generate a curve that darkens three-quartertones and brightens quartertones slightly. **(c)** The histograms for low-key images are weighted toward the left, representing the darker tones. To bring out detail in the shadows of such images, generate a concave curve that brightens three-quartertones, midtones, and quartertones.*

printed detail in such images, it often helps to darken the midtones and three-quarter-tones, leaving the quartertones unaltered.

- *Midtone* or *balanced* images, in which details of interest are either distributed evenly from dark to light or are concentrated in colors and tones of medium brightness, are the most common type you'll encounter. An "S"-shaped curve that darkens shadow detail and brightens highlight detail slightly helps emphasize midtone values. You may need to brighten or darken midtone values depending on the content and exposure of the original and on the amount of dot gain you expect.

- *Low-key* images feature the most important details in darker areas, with less emphasis on subjects in midtones and highlights. Photos of city scenes after dark are good examples of low-key images. You can improve detail in the shadows of such images by creating a concave curve to lighten quartertones, midtones, and three-quartertones.

Tonal distribution is unique for every image, so remember to modify these general guidelines to fit specific image requirements.

Tip: When working with a color image, you should apply some types of tonal correction to the composite image and some types to individual channels. Work with the composite color image when making adjustments based on image key, when correcting exposure problems, and when compensating for dot gain. Perform highlight and shadow adjustments and color balancing on a channel-by-channel basis.

Correcting Exposure Problems

The foregoing guidelines about tonal character assume that the unenhanced version is perfectly *exposed*—in other words, that brightness levels throughout the image are appropriate for emphasizing the details in the important subject areas. When the chief subject matter of an image lacks detail because it's too dark, it's *underexposed*; when it lacks detail because it's too light, it's *overexposed*.

Exposure problems can occur either because of a poor original or because of poor scanning or digitizing techniques, but you often can correct them through curve adjustments. To correct for underexposure, create a concave curve that dips deeply in the tonal range occupied by the important subject matter (use an eyedropper tool to determine this range). For example, if the chief details of interest in an underexposed image occupy the 70 to 90 percent range as in the example in Figure 7–4, generate a curve that dips in that area. Similarly, you can correct for overexposure by creating a convex curve in which the top of the "dome" corresponds to the tonal range occupied by the important subject matter.

Note: When an image is overexposed, detail has been lost that you can't recover. Corrections only improve the general balance of detail in the image; they can't manufacture detail that isn't there to start with.

When correcting exposure problems, keep in mind the relationship between curve shape, contrast, and detail. Making a curve more concave, as when correcting for underexposure, increases both contrast *and* apparent noise or film grain. Making a curve more convex, as when correcting for overexposure, reduces contrast and apparent graininess. (These rules assume that the curve values in your image-editing package progress from light at the left to dark at the right. If they progress from dark to light, the opposite is true.)

Figure 7–4

© Emil Ihrig

Use a concave curve to correct for underexposure and a convex curve to correct for overexposure. The bowl of a concave curve or the dome of a convex curve should correspond to the tonal range occupied by the most important subject matter— in these examples, the skin tones in the underexposed image (top) and the detail in the plaster cat's head for the overexposed image (bottom). You can anchor those parts of the curve that already have acceptable contrast relationships, to keep them from further manipulations that would lead to a loss in quality.

Print Output and Tonal Compression

The limitations of the printing process require that you compress the tonal range of images at the extremes of bright and dark and then make adjustments to the midtones to compensate for that compression. When you fail to compress the range of brightness levels at the extremes, detail drops out in light areas and plugs up in dark ones once ink is applied on press. When you compress the tonal range but neglect to adjust other tonal ranges to compensate, the entire image looks flat (see Figure 7–5). Making both types of adjustments helps preserve contrast, crispness of detail, and the appearance of lifelike color in print.

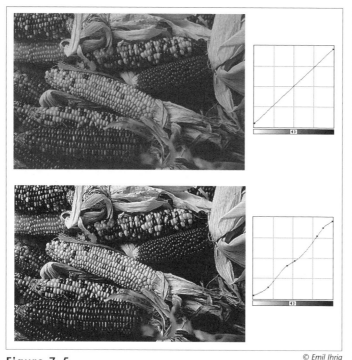

Figure 7–5

© Emil Ihrig

*Compressing the tonal range of an image prior to output prevents detail dropout at the extremes **(top)**, but you must then adjust other tonal ranges **(bottom)** to prevent a flat look and to optimize contrast and detail relationships*

Adjusting Highlight Values

Your first task in preparing an image for print output after converting it to CMYK should be to locate the highlight—the lightest area that should still print with detail. In an image that contains a pure white shirt, for example, the highlight might well be located in a fold or crease, where just a minimum of visible detail is present. If the highlight for a particular image falls in the diffuse highlight tones, you should adjust the curve(s) to the minimum highlight value recommended by your print vendor. A different strategy is required for images that contain no true highlights, as we'll see shortly.

The highlight value to which you should adjust an image depends on the press setup. As a general rule, higher-speed presses and uncoated papers can't hold a very small halftone dot, so highlight values for jobs that use them tend to be higher—usually in the neighborhood of 4 to 10 percent. Coated papers, especially when teamed with sheet-fed presses, can hold smaller dots—typically in the 3 to 5 percent range, though some high-quality stocks printed on sheet-fed presses can hold dots as small as 1 percent. There are plenty of variables, so ask your print vendor for specific recommendations.

Keep in mind that for color images, the respective highlight values will differ for each channel and you'll need to set them separately, rather than in the composite as with grayscale images. The cyan value will be several percentage points higher than the magenta and yellow values. Imagine that you're quoted a highlight value of 4 percent, for example. If your document will be printed on coated stock using GCR with light black generation, a 300 percent total ink limit, and an 85 percent black ink limit, then 4 percent will translate to minimum CMYK values of 4C2M2Y0K. *Memorize the CMY highlight values for your particular project.* Create a stepped grayscale that includes the minimum dot value, as described in the "Gray Balance: Neutral Is Not Equal" sidebar in Chapter 6. Convert the grayscale to CMYK using the correct color separation parameters, and then write down and apply the resulting CMY component values for the highlight.

Using Preset Curves

Adobe Photoshop and other leading image-editing packages allow you to create custom curves, save them, and then load them for later reuse. This level of automation is convenient, but avoid the temptation to use preset curves in a cookie-cutter fashion. There are a few functions for which automatic reapplication of custom curves makes sense: when correcting film emulsion characteristics for a large batch of photos from the same film, for example, or for dot gain correction for images that will be printed in the same document. But most of the time, you will have to make subtle changes to preset curves each time you load a different image, because every image is unique.

The best strategy is to master the *procedures* for adjusting curves on an image-by-image basis. Then, feel free to save several types of custom curves for each project—for example, a curve that compensates for a particular project's dot gain, or curves that set highlights, midtones, and shadows for high-key images, balanced images, and low-key images, respectively. But think of and use such preset curves as templates only—always make changes to the loaded curve as necessary to fit the content and other characteristics of the image at hand.

Curve shape is just as important as the highlight value itself. In most cases, you'll want to introduce an "S" shape into the part of the curve that represents the lightest tonal areas. This type of shape keeps the shifts between adjacent light tones looking natural to the eye and heightens contrast there. If you simply were to move the highlight value upward and leave the lower part of the curve as a diagonal line, on the other hand, the lightest tones in the image would appear dingy and flat. So when in doubt, keep the curve in the curve.

Finding the Highlight

Locating the highlight in an image is important for more reasons than one. In addition to helping you compress the tonal range accurately for print output, it can alert you to the presence of color casts that may not be detectible visually. See Chapter 8 for more on neutralizing color casts.

In single-subject grayscale images, you often can spot the highlight visually. But that's not typically the case for color images, where the presence of four different color values in each pixel can fool the eye. It's also difficult to spot the highlight in extremely detailed images. Rely on the numbers—use an eyedropper tool to compare values in light areas.

Tip: *If you use Adobe Photoshop on a Macintosh, you may be able to locate highlight values automatically. Open the Levels dialog box, making sure that the Preview option is deactivated, and press and hold the Option key while moving the highlight triangle. The screen goes white and as you move the slider, the pixels at the designated value show up in color, indicating exactly what subject areas the lightest values are located in. This technique also works for locating shadow values.*

Figure 7–6

© Emil Ihrig

Left: In normal images, the very lightest tones are located in the diffuse highlights (here, in the cloud formation marked by the black box) and should still print with detail. When you set the highlight value, the tail of the curve shifts upward slightly, and light values in the image become slightly darker. *Right:* Some parts of this woman's blouse are so bright that they may print as paper white. Minimum CMY values may remain at zero for images that contain specular highlights.

Specular Highlights

Some images contain subjects so brilliant that they need to print at the white point, brighter than the normal highlight value for the project would allow. It's perfectly acceptable, for example, to allow metallic glints from jewelry, sparks from industrial processes, areas featuring reflected glare, or pure whites to print without any detail at all (see Figure 7–6). Forcing these tones, called *specular highlights*, within normal compression limits would cause the entire image to look unnaturally dull. In these cases, leave the minimum CMY values at zero and don't adjust the tail of the curve upward at all. Instead, concentrate your adjustments on other

tonal areas of the image. For example, you might choose to darken the tones in the 5 to 15 percent range slightly to maximize contrast between the brilliant specular highlights and subjects that represent light details.

Images with No True Highlights

Low-key and some all-midtone images may contain few or no subjects in the lightest tonal areas, as the example in Figure 7–7 demonstrates (check with an eyedropper tool to make sure). In such cases, setting the lightest available tone to the normal highlight values for the project would shift existing values unnecessarily to darker tones and wash them out.

Leave the heel of the curve unaltered, but be aware that you'll need to focus on intensifying contrast and detail in the midtones and shadows, which may otherwise appear flat.

Tip: *If an image contains light pastels but no near-whites, use the pastels to set the highlight. Pastel color values typically fall within the 5 to 15 percent range; a light beige, for example, may have the values 5C5M15Y0K. Set the component highlight values in each channel separately. Familiarize yourself with the typical CMYK values of many different pastels and observe their CMY balances.*

When Highlights Contain a Color Cast

Because of the nonlinear way in which we perceive light, we're more likely to spot unrealistic tints in light tones than in dark ones. If your eyedropper tool detects a tone that should be a grayscale highlight but for which the values are seriously out of balance, a mental alarm should go off. A reading of 4C2M10Y, for example, indicates a yellow cast, which may or may not be readily apparent to the eye depending on the subject matter and the colors surrounding it. Lest you fall prey to the temptation to make a local selection and adjust just the offending subject matter, recall that any color imbalance in the highlights probably pervades other tonal regions as well. You may have to adjust the entire curve for the offending channel

© Emil Ihrig

Figure 7–7
Some images contain neither highlights nor speculars because their subjects are all in the midtones or darker tonal ranges. For such images, there's no need to remap the highlight value to anything higher than zero; doing so would cause existing values to shift unnecessarily darker.

(and other channels, too), not just the highlights. See Chapter 8 for examples and guidelines.

Of course, a yellow cast may be just fine if the color in question isn't supposed to be neutral. If the lightest color in an image is a pastel, for example, it wouldn't do to force it to a pale gray. By the same token, a near-white subject photographed at sunset would have a very warm highlight, which should *not* be neutralized. Let the subject matter and the lighting conditions of the original guide you when making decisions about whether to remap highlights to neutral values.

Adjusting Shadow Values

Between them, the highlight value and the shadow value define the maximum contrast range for an image. Locating the darkest area that should still print with detail is not an easy task for the eye, which finds it difficult to differentiate between dark colors or shades above the three-quartertones. Make sure you've done your color separation homework correctly with regard to limiting total ink coverage. In an image color separated using the parameters described in the "Adjusting Highlight Values" section earlier, the maximum value that will still hold detail is 96 percent, which translates to 80C68M67Y73K for a dark neutral gray (component channel values will vary for shadow areas that feature color rather than neutrals). Any color combination that sums to a higher combined number than this is suspect—if you want detail to be visible there, you need to adjust its values downward.

Tip: Night scenes and other low-key images can benefit from a shadow value even lower than the one recommended by your print vendor. They will also require a beefing up of contrast within the darker tonal ranges to bring out detail in the important subject areas.

Setting the Shadow Value

For a grayscale image, set the shadow value by adjusting the head of the curve down to the percentage specified by your print vendor, as in Figure 7–8. You're compressing the tonal range of the image, so you'll notice the darker tones shifting to slightly lighter values. For CMYK images, set the maximum shadow value in the composite color image if you want a neutral black, or channel by channel if you prefer to maintain control over a non-neutral black. (Low-key images often look more vibrant if the colors above the three-quartertones are *not* neutral.)

Figure 7–8   © Emil Ihrig

*If an image contains extremely dark tones above the printer-recommended maximum dot value, failing to adjust the shadow value downward causes those dark areas to plug up (**top**). Adjusting the shadow value downward with an "S"-curve shape preserves eye-pleasing contrast in the darker tones and opens up the darker details under the arch of the theatre marquee, in the reflective surfaces to the right of the walking couple, and in the "Town Square" sign above the striped awning (**bottom**).*

Curve shape is just as important as the shadow value itself. In most cases, you'll want to introduce an "S" shape into the curve. This type of shape keeps the shifts between adjacent dark tones looking natural to the eye and heightens contrast. If you simply moved the shadow value downward and left the upper curve area as a diagonal line, on the other hand, the darkest tones in the image would appear flat. Once again—when in doubt, keep the curve in the curve.

Images with No True Shadows

High-key and some midtone images contain few or no shadow values in the subjects of interest; therefore all grayscale or color values already fall well below the limits specified by the printer. In these cases, leave the head of the curve unaltered. Concentrate your curve adjustments on the midtone and lighter areas of the image to maximize contrast there.

Basic Midtone Adjustments

After you compress the tonal range at the extremes through highlight and shadow adjustments, it's important to make compensating adjustments to other areas of the curve as well. We'll call these other areas midtones, though in real-world projects you're just as likely to make changes to quartertones and three-quartertones, too. Midtone adjustments have three important benefits:

- They restore contrast and detail lost in the process of setting highlight and shadow values (compressing the tonal range).
- They bring out the best potential of the image based on tonal character.
- They compensate for anticipated dot gain.

Restoring Contrast Based on Tonal Character

The tonal character of an image, as described earlier in this chapter (see "Identifying Tonal Character" and Figure 7–3) can point you in the right direction regarding the best way to

optimize *all* tonal areas of an image, not just the highlights and shadows. Don't follow our guidelines slavishly, though—in their purest form, they apply only to images that have no color casts and in which important subjects already show optimum contrast, detail, and tonal emphasis. There's usually room for improvement even in the best of source images, so consider the guidelines as a springboard from which you can depart to do custom work. It bears repeating: every image is unique!

Curve-Based Dot Gain Compensation

Chapter 6 discusses the impact of dot gain on image quality; here, our concern is with how to adjust an image to compensate for the amount of dot gain you anticipate. As mentioned earlier, the tonal character of an image dictates the general shape of the curve adjustment you should make in the midtones (such as concave or convex). Once you know the anticipated amount of dot gain as quoted by your print vendor, use your knowledge of an image's tonal character to help you determine the *extent* to which you need to compensate for that dot gain, if at all. Midtone and low-key images have an abundance of subject matter in the tonal ranges most likely to be heavily impacted by dot gain, so it's especially important to lighten their midtone values. How much should you lighten them? Good question. There are no easily accessible mathematical formulas for calculating how to make a lighter dot print as a 50 percent dot (dots lighter than 50 percent are subject to lower dot gain amounts than the midtones themselves). Some software programs do part of the calculation work for you in the background. If you use Adobe Photoshop, for example, a good method is to define a dot gain amount in Printing Inks Setup and then adjust the midtones and darker tones visually until these critical areas appear light enough. As in

Figure 7–9

© Emil Ihrig

Top: This image, adjusted for highlight and shadow extremes only, suffers from heavy dot gain in the midtones and darker areas and a consequent loss of visible detail. Bottom: After dot gain adjustment, the barrel rings and the foliage in the upper-right corner are opened up to preserve detail and maintain good contrast relationships. The appropriate curve shape to compensate for dot gain depends on the tonal ranges occupied by the subject matter you want to emphasize.

Figure 7–9, keep the curve shapely to retain eye-pleasing contrast relationships.

High-key images, which contain few subjects in the midtone or darker ranges, may not require dot gain compensation adjustments. In fact, with high-key images it may even be beneficial to increase midtone values, since contrast between highlight tones and available midtones should be maximized.

Tip: *When adjusting the midtones of color images specifically to compensate for dot gain, adjust the composite image. Adjusting on a channel-by-channel basis could introduce color casts unless you're an expert color separator. Remember, too, that adjusting the midtones also alters adjacent tonalareas. Anchor the parts of the curve that you want to protect from further adjustment.*

Jobs printed using stochastic and FM screening technologies are subject to higher dot gain amounts than jobs that use halftone screening (see Chapter 3). Dot gain of up to 35 percent isn't uncommon. If your job will be using FM screening, be sure to work with a print vendor who has experience with the technology and can specify the correct amount of dot gain for which you should compensate.

Tone into Color

There's no limit to the number of tone curve shapes you can concoct to improve color, contrast, and detail in both grayscale and color images. That's where the lines of demarcation between tonal and color correction start to blur—rapidly. Considerations such as color cast, intensification of hue, and the sacrifice of some tonal ranges to gain leverage in others begin to assume an importance equal to that of correcting for basic print reproduction limitations, and *voilà*—we're in the realm of color correction techniques, the subject of Chapter 8.

8

Balancing and Correcting Color

Digital image-editing tools bring precision to the process of adjusting color for output. Whether you're editing curves, altering hue or saturation values, or blending multiple channels, you can improve on the raw material of an image with an exactness that traditional methods can't match. Digital tools let you match the color of high-quality originals (when matching is the goal) or coax the potentials out of less-than-stellar images.

Ever since desktop technology began to democratize the process of image editing, terminology has been getting dangerously watered down. We throw around the term "color correction," for example, with a looseness that makes traditional color separation professionals wince. We owe it to the integrity of this highly precise field to be less sloppy. Technically speaking, digital color adjustments fall into two general categories: color balancing and color correction.

■ *Color balancing* refers to all the adjustments you can make in the RGB or CMYK color space using curves, levels, and other tools that let you manipulate tonal levels on a channel-by-channel basis. Color-balancing techniques *do* alter individual colors, but in a way that affects other colors in the image as well. Using tone curves, for example, you can't actually remove

113

or add absolute amounts of a given color any more than you can take rubber out of a rubber band. You can only stretch the rubber band so that it becomes more or less taut. In the same way, curves and other color-balancing tools only let you *redistribute* colors in an image. Of course, redistribution makes its own magic, letting you disguise color you don't want by tucking it into tonal ranges where the eye doesn't notice it or concentrate color you do want in areas where it shows off to best advantage.

■ *Color correction* properly refers only to manipulations that alter a color without affecting any other colors—actually subtracting some red, green, or yellow from a picture, for example. Such adjustments can only be made in a luminance-based color space, such as HLS, or using tools that simulate HLS-type adjustments (such as the Hue/Saturation, Replace Color, or Selective Color controls in Adobe Photoshop).

We'll devote the rest of this chapter to an exploration of the most common color adjustments you encounter on a day-to-day basis: grappling with color casts, giving proper emphasis to important colors and subjects, cleansing murky colors, toning down overly brilliant colors, refining contrast and contouring with the help of the unwanted (gray component) color, and exact color matching.

The Ground Rules

Every scientist must record his or her assumptions when conducting an experiment, and we want to be equally candid when advising you on methods for adjusting color. Here are the ground rules we follow throughout this chapter:

1. *Avoid the temptation to select and manipulate limited areas of an image.* Often, if a color doesn't look right in one range, there are problems with that color throughout the image. Adjusting the entire image will fix not only the obvious problems, but also the ones the eye doesn't notice as readily. (If an image truly requires local correction, you should handle it after adjusting the image as a whole.)

2. *Make adjustments on a channel-by-channel basis.* Making corrections globally doesn't mean adjusting the composite color image. You'll usually obtain the best results by correcting each component channel individually. You often can fix color and detail problems by adjusting values in a single channel—for example, the black channel, the channel complementary to the color cast (cyan for red problems), or the channel in which detail is most lacking. When the challenge is more complex, tweaking each channel in a different way may yield the most perfect version.

3. *Work in the optimum color space.* Most of the time this will be CMYK for color balancing (or RGB with CMYK preview if you don't yet have the necessary information to commit your pixels to CMYK). For true color-correction adjustments, you can work best in HLS, unless you use an application that allows you to make HLS-type adjustments while still in CMYK or RGB mode.

4. *Every image is unique.* With tools like custom preset curves at your disposal, it's tempting to overuse them. But to the extent that subject matter, lighting conditions, color content, and digitization method vary from one image to the next, the color adjustments required for each image will, too. Save any number of preset curves, but regard them as templates that you should alter manually in

a different way for each image. The only exception to this rule is if all the images for your publication feature the same subjects captured under controlled lighting conditions, such as studio shots of a single product line.

Neutralizing Color Casts

Raster images fall into two categories: *photorealistic images*, in which believable, true-to-life colors are essential, and *original illustrations*, in which the colors of the imagination often take precedence over realistic color. One of your most important tasks when you enhance photorealistic images is to determine whether there are any unwanted color casts and, if so, to neutralize them.

A *color cast* is any undesirable tint that pervades an image (or even limited tonal ranges of an image). The key word is *undesirable*. Some color casts, such as the warm yellow-red apparent in photographs taken shortly before sunset, help create an atmosphere and enhance visual appeal. So don't assume that you should blindly zap every cast you detect; consider the subject matter and the use to which each image will be put in your publication. If a cast might help convey a message, keep it.

Detecting Color Casts

Before you can neutralize a color cast, you first have to locate one. Many color casts are easy to spot visually, if you just know where to look. Typically, casts are most obvious in subjects that appear in neutrals, in diffuse highlights, or in memory colors. But never rely on the eye alone; take an eyedropper or onscreen densitometer reading to be sure.

> **"***Don't assume that you should blindly zap every cast you detect; consider the subject matter and the use to which each image will be put in your publication.***"**

Casts in Neutrals

When evaluating an image for potential color casts, look first for neutral subjects—especially whites or lighter shades of gray—since the eye is most sensitive to casts in lighter subjects. Your chief ally in this quest is a gray balance chart, which you should create for each project and which will provide you with CMYK equivalents of grayscale values throughout the printable tonal range (see the "Gray Balance: Neutral Is Not Equal" sidebar in Chapter 6).

If an image contains subjects that should print as specular highlights—either absolutely white or as glittering reflections with no detail—CMY values should all be at zero. Survey the subject's values with an eyedropper tool; cyan, magenta, or yellow values well above the highlight value in a subject that should print as a specular indicates that a color cast is present. In Figure C–15 in the Color Gallery, for example, the values for the artificial snow in the jeweler's window, which should be white, are indicative of a red cast that can best be addressed by adjustments to both the magenta and yellow channels (magenta and yellow combine to produce red). The "Cast Correction: A Color-Balancing Strategy" section of this chapter describes one way to neutralize this cast.

Tip: *A cast in one tonal range probably affects other tonal ranges as well. Avoid selecting just the offending subject and adjusting its color alone. The exception to this rule is the cross curve induced by film-processing chemistry, in which casts of complementary colors—magenta and green, for example—appear at opposite extremes of the tonal range.*

When examining gray subjects in a color image, don't trust the eye alone; surrounding colors could corrupt the eye's perception of neutrality. Survey the intended grayscale subjects with an eyedropper and then compare their values to the gray balance chart for your project. If the balance between cyan and magenta or yellow varies much from the values in the chart, the color in the image is definitely lopsided.

Casts in Highlights

Images that contain no neutral subjects may be inconvenient if you're looking for an easy way to spot color casts, but all is not lost. If an image contains at least some diffuse highlights (see Chapter 7), you're still likely to spot any lurking culprits visually, since casts are more obvious to the eye when present in lighter subjects. Pastels, for example, aren't neutral—a beige contains more yellow than cyan and magenta, and a light blue contains much more cyan and magenta than yellow—but with experience, you can easily get a feel for the direction in which any given light color is *supposed* to shift. Double-check your visual perception with an eyedropper reading.

Casts in Memory Colors

What if an image contains neither neutrals nor diffuse highlights? No problem. Most visuals include one or more universally recognizable colors, called *memory colors*—familiar subjects such as grass, sky, flesh tones, animals, or common food items such as meats, fruits, and vegetables. Because we know what these colors should look like, the eye immediately perceives any shifts toward another hue.

Following are "ballpark" color specifications for some common memory colors. It's important to recognize that with memory colors, it's the *ratios* between the CMY primaries, not their absolute values, that matters most. Even with exact matches, actual values can vary slightly from one image to another without being casted, since every color can be expressed using many different combinations of CMYK inks. There are plenty of other memory colors, of course; you can familiarize yourself with them by observing the exact color values of examples in uncasted images.

- *Sky blue*—60C23M0Y0K. Magenta should not exceed 40 percent of the cyan value; once it does, the blue begins to take on a violet cast.

- *Lemon yellow*—5C18M75Y0K. More magenta leads to a reddish cast; more cyan, to a dulling of the yellow.

- *Caucasian flesh tones*—18C45M50Y0K. There's quite a bit of leeway here. Magenta and yellow always remain basically equal (yellow only 0 to 20 percent higher than magenta), with lower values for paler skin. Cyan gives a tanned look to skin but should not be greater than 40 percent of the yellow.

- *Oriental flesh tones*—15C40M55Y0K. Yellow can be higher in proportion to magenta than with Caucasian flesh tones.

- *Black flesh tones*—35C45M50Y28K. Once again, cyan browns the skin, but the relationship between magenta and yellow remains more or less equal.

The colors in Figure C–16 in the Color Gallery look beautifully saturated—until you take a closer look at the skin tones, which exhibit a blue cast that's also visible (though less obviously so) in the clothing. Neutralizing the image requires shifting color away from blue and toward its complement, yellow; we'll examine one way to do this in the "Cast Correction: A Color-Correction Strategy" section later in this chapter.

Detecting Subtle Casts

Not all color casts are obvious to the unaided eye. You'll probably spot a cast if the imbalance occurs in a white or grayscale subject, in a memory color, or in the main subject of an image *if* that subject is light in color. However, you're not likely to detect casts visually in cases of subordinate subjects, small subjects, subjects in the midtone or darker color ranges, subjects surrounded by vividly contrasting colors, or subjects surrounded by multicolored details. For images containing those kinds of subjects, your surest recourse is to survey the entire image with an eyedropper, looking for neutrals and memory colors as reliable reference points.

Neutralizing Casts

Before taking steps to neutralize a color cast that you have detected in an image, ask yourself whether the offending colors (white, grays, or whatever) really need to be neutral in the printed version. This is a subjective judgment; there's no single "right" answer for all cases.

Neither is there one "right" way to neutralize a cast. We'll present two basic methods here: a color-balancing technique that uses curve adjustments affecting all colors and a color-correction technique that impacts only a limited set of colors. Each is preferable in certain circumstances. Regardless of which technique you use, most cases don't require that you make a local selection to correct just the subject in which the cast is most evident. Adjusting color throughout in multiple channels throughout the image usually yields much better results, cleaning up contrast and detail problems that you might not otherwise recognize as related.

Tip: You can use the techniques described here to intensify casts as well as neutralize them, if the concept of your publication calls for it.

Cast Correction: A Color-Balancing Strategy

Frequently, a cast is at its most offensive in limited brightness ranges only, and it wouldn't do to reduce the color evenly throughout the image. For cases like these, global CMYK curve adjustments may be the most effective way to neutralize a color cast. Curves offer a great deal of control over both the amount of color change and the tonal ranges you alter.

The original image of the items in a jeweler's window (Figure C–15 in the Color Gallery) contains a blatant red cast, probably the result of using outdoor film to photograph items in an indoor case under incandescent lighting. The diffuse highlights in the artificial snow, which should be off-white, read out as a clearly unbalanced C18M48Y53K2, and the colors of the necklace don't stand out from the background. A bit of prepress color logic makes our choice of strategy easy. We know these things:

- The colors magenta and yellow compose red on press, so both colors must be excessive to bring about so pronounced a cast. A look at the dark original magenta and yellow channels in Figure 8–1 confirms this surmise.

- An eyedropper survey reveals that the cast is most egregious in the highlights, quartertones, and midtones. Magenta and yellow read out as 45 to 70 percent in areas where they should be only 5 to 30 percent! Reducing the amounts of magenta and yellow in the lighter tonal ranges means that we'll have to allow much more of those colors in the shadows, but that's all right; stretching the rubber band this way will strengthen contrast throughout the image.

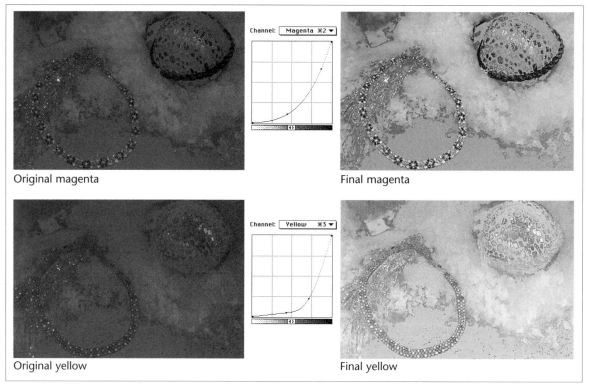

Original magenta

Final magenta

Original yellow

Final yellow

Figure 8–1

© Emil Ihrig

*Correcting a strongly red-casted white requires curve adjustments to the magenta and yellow channels to reduce the amounts of those colors in the highlights, quartertones, and midtones and strengthen contrast at the extremes of the tonal range. **Left to right:** the original magenta and yellow channels, the correction curves for magenta and yellow, and the final magenta and yellow channels. Figure C–15 in the Color Gallery contains the original and revised versions of the color images.*

■ The cyan channel can also help achieve the goal of neutralizing the cast, since cyan kills red. In the case of this image, a slight boost of cyan in the quartertones and between the midtones and the shadows is all that's needed to suppress the red once magenta and yellow have been adjusted, so we didn't include the unimpressive-looking cyan curve.

The curves accompanying the channels in Figure 8–1 show how we carried out the planned strategy. We reduced magenta through the midtones and reduced yellow even more severely, all the way to the 60 percent range. (The yellow channel was even flatter and more saturated in the original image.) The resulting steepening of both curves through the three-quarter tones and shadows added definition and "punch" to the subject matter. In the final image, the jewelry leaps out from its background, and the snow is recognizable as snow.

Combining Color-Balancing and Color-Correction Strategies

Figure C–17 in the Color Gallery, a low-key dusk scene, shows another kind of cast in neutrals. This image is a classic example of *cross curve* casting: The drive-in pillars and sidewalk, which should be off-white and medium gray, respectively, evidence a strong green cast (introduced by the interaction between film and the fluorescent lighting at the drive-in), while the darker sunset sky is too unbelievably magenta. Cross-curve casts are sometimes difficult to eliminate using global curve adjustments alone, precisely because they occur in complementary colors and in different tonal ranges; in the process of neutralizing a cast in one tonal range, curve adjustments can cause subjects in other tonal ranges to shift even more drastically toward the complementary color. To neutralize all casts completely without introducing new color distortions, this image required supplementing color balancing techniques with color-correction measures.

- The green cast in the highlights and quartertones was the highest priority for us to neutralize, since the eye perceives color casts most easily in light subjects. We used a color-balancing strategy, reducing cyan and yellow (which compose green on press) in the highlights, quartertones, and midtones. We had to reduce the amount of yellow draconically (see Figure 8–2). Increasing magenta through the midtones neutralized the green cast in the lighter ranges even further. The unusual "double-dipping" shape of the magenta curve was necessary to preserve intense color in the marquees. Increasing black through the quartertones protected the pavement and pillars from further casting.

- As the center image in Figure C–17 shows, the color-balancing strategy of using global curve adjustments improved the image but could-not perfect it. We had to limit the amount of yellow we removed from the lighter tonal ranges to keep the canopies from turning blatantly magenta. But as a result, a yellow cast still remained in the pavement and pillars, and the canopies shifted away from red and toward magenta anyway. The magenta that we had to preserve in the midtones

made the sky even more starkly magenta than before, with no yellow to tone it down.

- To complete the job, we resorted to HLS-type color adjustments and local selections. Photoshop's Color Range command allowed us to select all of the red marquee canopies quickly and intuitively. We then used the Selective Color command to add enough yellow to these areas to restore their original true red color. Finally, to neutralize the excess magenta in the sky, we used the Color Range and Selective Color commands once again to select large areas of the sky and add cyan and black. The final version of the image in Figure C–17 shows the result.

Cast Correction: A Color-Correction Strategy

Curve adjustments are marvelous when you prefer to limit your changes to specific tonal ranges. If, however, a cast permeates multiple tonal ranges evenly and your main goal is *reduce* the overall amount of the cast color or change it to a different color, curves can't work magic; using hue-based adjustment tools serves the purpose more efficiently. Take the vineyard image in Figure C–16 in the Color Gallery, for example. The subject is in the shade, which pushes the image toward blue. Anomalies in film emulsion and development deepen the blue cast further, as does the coloration of the clothing reflecting off the subject's face. The ratio of cyan to magenta in the skin tones is 66 percent, far above normal. To shift all blues universally toward their complement, yellow, and to brighten the image as a whole, we adjusted numerical values for all cyans, blues, and magentas in the image using Photoshop's Selective Color controls, as shown in Figure 8–3. HLS-type adjustments don't just flex the rubber band of color like curve adjustments do; they actually add isolated colors to or subtract them from an image without altering other colors.

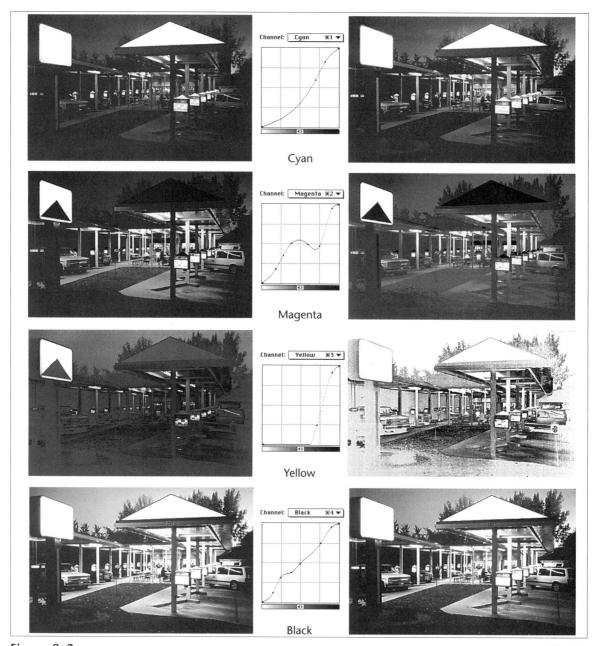

Figure 8–2

© Emil Ihrig

*The original image in Figure C–17 has a green cast in the highlights and quartertones and a complementary magenta cast in the midtone-to-shadow range (a cross-curve cast). As the center image in Figure C–17 shows, the use of curve adjustments alone offers only a partial solution; substantially neutralizing the green cast in the highlights only aggravates the complementary magenta cast in the midtones. Comparing the original channels (**left**), the curves used to reduce the green cast (**center**), and the resulting channels (**right**) shows how curves compromised the image and why additional color correction was necessary.*

Color Casts: Summing Up

Here are important points to keep in mind when evaluating and correcting color casts.

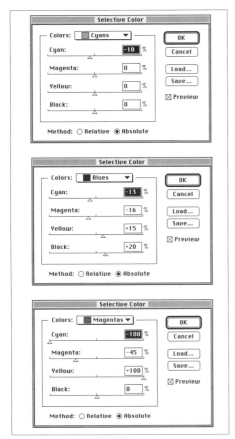

Figure 8–3

HLS-type adjustments can eliminate pervasive color casts by changing the hue, saturation, or lightness values of isolated colors in an image. To reduce the overall amount of blue in Figure C–16 in the Color Gallery and shift the image toward a warmer yellow, we made global reductions to the amount of cyan in all cyans, blues, and magentas; global reductions to the amount of magenta in all blues and magentas; and global increases to the amount of yellow in all blues and magentas.

- Look for and measure reference points—neutrals first and memory colors second.

- Be alert to the possibility that more than one channel may contribute to the cast.

- To neutralize a cast, look to the channel that represents the color complementary to it. Magenta kills green; cyan kills red; and yellow kills blue.

- Many casts are strongest in specific tonal ranges. Flattening a curve to reduce a color in one range means you'll have to steepen the curve for that color in some other range. Pick that other range carefully, if possible making it one where very little of the color is used or in a dark area where the color won't be obvious. Use a grayscale color balance chart to check results.

- When you need to alter an offending color in isolation from others, consider using HLS-type adjustments.

- To help minimize casts in neutral grays and in three-quarter or shadow tones, optimize the black channel and choose color separation settings carefully.

Enhancing Important Colors and Subjects

Improvements to the printable color of a digital image can take many forms beyond just eliminating color casts. There's a whole array of color manipulations you can perform to heighten the appearance of detail, increase contrast or color saturation, tone down overly brilliant colors, or enliven dull ones. The tools that achieve these ends are the ones you've already seen in this chapter and in Chapter 6, and the common aim of these adjustments is to enhance the most important colors and subjects.

Whatever your aim in enhancing color, it's good practice to begin by surveying the image with an eyedropper tool to determine channel-by-channel color distribution. Jot down both the tonal ranges in which each color is most prominent and the tonal ranges in which each color is used least. If you'll be using curves to make color adjustments, this information will help you decide how to emphasize color in important subject areas at the expense of color in less important areas. If you use HLS-type adjustments to shift colors, a preliminary survey alerts you to areas that have a common color content so that you can plan the best strategy for altering isolated colors.

Boosting Contrast and Detail

When image quality is basically acceptable and all you want to do is bring out latent potentials, you need to make only subtle adjustments.

One common enhancement involves improving contrast and/or detail. Sharpening is neither the only nor even necessarily the most effective tool for pumping added contrast and detail into a milky or dull image. Adeptly shaped curves can boost contrast where it's needed most, heighten clarity of detail wherever you want to draw the eye, and intensify the colors of important subjects into the bargain. Take the original photo in Figure C–18 in the Color Gallery. There's nothing really wrong with this image, although the shade and the time of day emphasize blues. But wouldn't the image have even more visual pep if the flag were redder and the grain of the wood stood out?

As Figure 8–4 shows, making these subtle adjustments was straightforward.

- We flattened cyan from the highlights through the midtones (where it dampened the red of the already-faded flag) and strengthened it in the shadow tones, where it intensified the blue in the flag.

- We boosted magenta amounts between the midtone and three-quarter tones to benefit saturation and contouring in the flag, its reflection, and the play of light on the wood.

- We pulled back yellow through the quarter-tones and midtones, where it weakened the red of the flag.

- We increased black strongly in the quarter-tones and in the shadows to boost contrast in many important subjects of the image.

Tip: Converting an image to LAB color and then generating an "S"-curve in the L (luminance) channel is another way to add sparkle to an image. See Chapter 10 for examples.

Intensifying Saturation

When an image is to be used in advertising, it needs to have as much emotional appeal as possible. That requirement often translates into the demand for colors that pop—that are as intense, as brilliant, and as saturated as possible. For high-budget print jobs, the use of HiFi color separations, waterless presses, stochastic screening, and expensive coated papers may help meet this goal; but even if you're working with CMYK channels, you can intensify color saturation using your choice of techniques.

The original garden scene in Figure C–19 in the Color Gallery could be even more delectable if only the color of the grass and pad on the wicker chair were more vivid. There is more than one way to approach this challenge. We could, for example, make curve adjustments, doing much of the work in the magenta channel since the primary subject colors are complementary (magenta and green). But since our primary goal in this case is to make colors more vivid, we can use luminance-based HLS-type adjustments and encumber ourselves with fewer acrobatic gyrations. Increasing saturation in the greens and saturation and lightness in the magentas helped us arrive at the snappier final version in Figure C–19.

Controlling Brilliance and Depth

A color image in which *all* of the subjects are light and bright seems to lack depth as well as detail. At the other extreme, an otherwise colorful image that has too much darkness woven

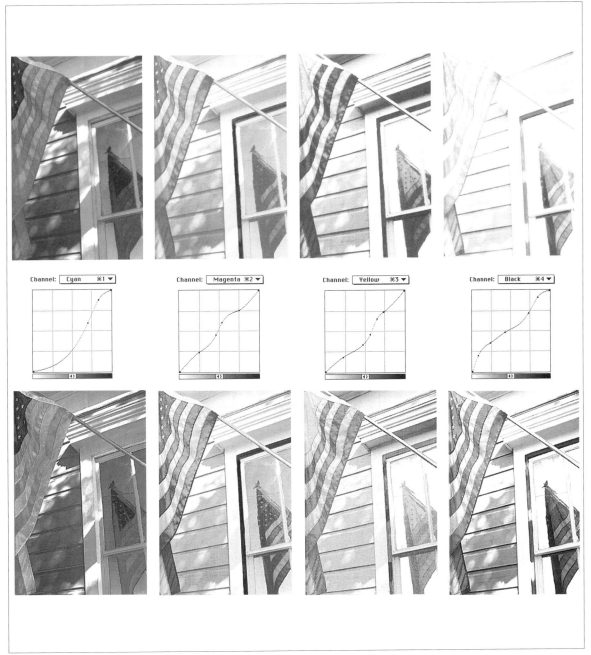

© Emil Ihrig

Figure 8–4

Subtle curve adjustments in an otherwise acceptable image can bring out latent detail and improve contrast and saturation. **Top to bottom:** *The original CMYK channels for the original image in Figure C–18 in the Color Gallery, curve adjustments for each channel, and the final (adjusted) channels.*

throughout its fabric can appear muddy. The black channel, together with channel blending and duplication techniques, are among your most important allies in controlling brilliance and depth. Let's look at a couple of examples to prove the point.

Giving Depth to Overly Brilliant Colors

Yes, you thought that we print professionals were supposed to spend most of our time trying to intensify colors, not tone them down. But neither do we want a washout. The original tropical cocktails in Figure C–20 in the Color Gallery almost hurt the eyes with their out-of-balance brightness. A survey with an eyedropper reveals that the chief subjects are all light, bright yellow or orange and that except for the background, there's hardly any black to be found anywhere—certainly not enough to provide good detail. To give this image the appearance of greater depth, we would need to make detail stand out in the foam and the pineapple, intensify contrast between the cherry and its background, and create better contouring for the rim of the background glass. Curves alone can't make these things happen, because curves can't manufacture something out of nothing. Instead, we chose to work a little magic—the abracadabra of channel blending and alternative methods of color separation (see Figure 8–5). Here's the strategy that worked well for this case:

1. Since the original color image featured such a sorry excuse for a black channel, we decided to generate a second set of color separations. We duplicated the image, converted the duplicate to LAB color temporarily, and then converted it back to CMYK using GCR with a heavy black and no UCA. The resulting set of separations showed slightly more to work

with in the black channel and less density in the other three channels.

2. To engineer even more raw material into the black channel in this second set of separations, we created a new black channel that blended 89 percent of the heavier black channel with just 11 percent of the yellow channel. Allowing just a small amount of the yellow channel to be blended gave us the benefit of richer detailing without the extreme density that the yellow channel shows. (Too much density in the manufactured black channel would make everything murky.)

3. We substituted the newly manufactured black (blended) channel for the original one in the second set of separations. This step immediately improved depth in the foam of the foreground beverage, but the increased black in the image dulled the orange color in the background beverage more than was desirable, so we still had more work to do.

4. To restore the warmth of the orange, we increased the amount of magenta in the midtones only.

5. As a final touch, we increased black in the quartertones to provide stronger contouring in the light areas.

Figure 8–5 shows how we carried out the most important of these steps.

Cleansing Muddy Colors

The original image in Figure C–21 in the Color Gallery suffers from a problem exactly opposite to the one described in the previous section: there's too much darkness muddying up the otherwise colorful detail. To gently clean off the mud so that the colors of the lead crystal could shine forth as in the final example in Figure C–21, we used a combination of techniques that are similar to the ones used for Figure

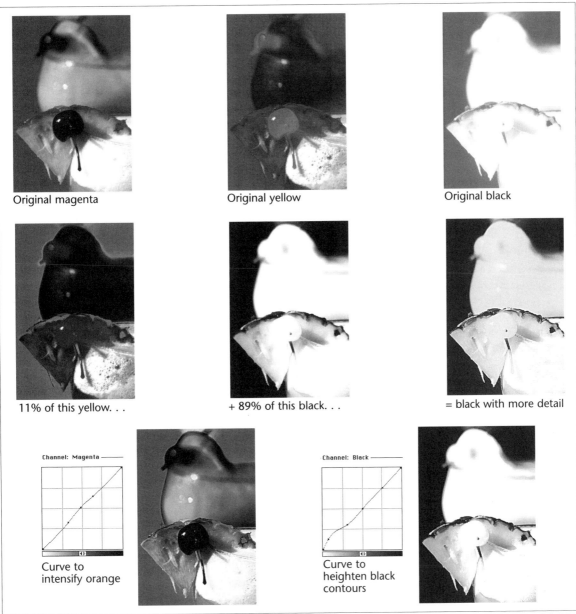

Original magenta

Original yellow

Original black

11% of this yellow. . .

+ 89% of this black. . .

= black with more detail

Channel: Magenta

Curve to
intensify orange

Channel: Black

Curve to
heighten black
contours

© Emil Ihrig

Figure 8–5

*To tone down the overly brilliant color in the original image in Figure C–20 in the Color Gallery and provide more depth, a combination of channel blending and curve adjustment techniques saved the day. **Top:** The original magenta, yellow, and black channels; note the extreme density in the yellow and the lack of detail in the black. **Center:** After creating a second set of separations to generate a heavier black, blending just a small amount of the new yellow channel with the new black channel created an even better black channel with better detailing. **Bottom:** Intensifying the magenta midtones and increasing the black quartertone in the manufactured black channel restored color and improved contouring.*

C–20. Here's a step-by step outline that you may find useful for similar cases:

1. If the original image is in RGB mode, separate it into CMYK channels using GCR with UCA so that more weight is given to the primary colors than to black. In our example image, the greatest amount of work needs to be done in the yellow and black channels; the original yellow channel (Figure 8-6a) is heavy and flat, and there's simply too much black for the colorful look we want (Figure 8-6b).

2. Duplicate the original CMYK image.

3. Temporarily convert the duplicate image to LAB or CIE color. Then set up new color separation parameters—GCR (no UCA), heavy black generation, and a black ink limit of 80 percent. Reconvert the duplicate image to CMYK. The new color separation settings have the effect of lightening the three primary channels—especially critical for yellow (Figure 8-6c).

4. Blend the old and new versions of the flattest color channel (yellow, in our case) to generate a new channel that's somewhat lighter and offers more contrast than the original (Figure 8-6d). The percentage of the blend will vary depending on the condition of the image at hand.

5. Substitute the newly manufactured (blended) channel for its counterpart in the original separations. In our case, the new yellow channel warms up the picture as it brightens up the color.

6. Turn your attention to the black channel, where much of the magic takes place. Create a copy of the original, more contrasty black channel and jettison all the black below a given percentage (12 percent, in our case). This throws out the black that's blocking the brighter colors.

7. Adjust the curve of this copy of the original black channel to lighten all the remaining blacks (effectively increasing the black gamma), *except* in the darkest ranges, where a gentle "S"-curve can heighten contrast in the shadows. Figure 8-6e shows how this curve (jettisoned black highlights and all) looked for our example, and Figure 8-6f shows the resulting black channel.

8. Finally, substitute the altered version of the original black channel for the one in the duplicate separations and increase black slightly in the quartertones to improve edge definition. The result in Figure C–21 in the Color Gallery speaks for itself: Tiffanys with a decidedly more shimmering glow.

Making the Most of the "Underdog" Color

Yin and yang, light and shadow, magenta and green—opposites, it seems, are always mutually dependent and intertwined. Nowhere is this rule of thumb more important to remember than in the field of digital color correction. In any given image color, two of the CMY inks predominate, and the third color is considered the unwanted color. (We like to call it the "underdog" color.) Don't let the nomenclature fool you; the unwanted color delivers power into your hands (or mouse!), giving you the same type of control over contrast and detail that we normally associate with the black channel. For example,

■ Steepening the curve of a complementary color channel improves definition in colors and images that otherwise would appear flat.

(a) Original yellow channel   (b) Original black channel   (c) Duplicate (GCR) yellow channel

(d) Blended yellow channel

Channel: Black

(e) Curve to jettison highlight blacks

(f) Final black channel

© Emil Ihrig

Figure 8–6

Channel blends and substitutions play a key role in brightening the murky original in Figure C–21. (a) The original yellow channel is heavy and poorly detailed. (b) The original black channel shows great detail and contouring but blocks too much of the color in the lighter tonal ranges. (c) This new, lighter, yellow channel results from creating a duplicate set of separations using heavy black generation with no UCA. (d) Blending the original and duplicate yellow channels results in a less heavy version with better contrast, which is then substituted for the yellow channel in the duplicate set of separations. (e) Applying this curve to a copy of the original black channel eliminates black from the lightest tonal ranges while retaining good shadow contouring. (f) The lightened version of the original black channel is substituted for the one in the duplicate set of separations.

- Reducing the unwanted color in dingy tonal ranges of an image brightens the colors there, often more effectively than if you simply increased the amounts of the dominant colors.

- Overly brilliant colors can be toned down effectively by a judicious increase of the unwanted or complementary color.

Caution: *Reducing the unwanted color also eliminates some detail. In a photo of a red barn, for example, reducing cyan content results in loss of subtle detail in the grain of the wood, which cyan as the unwanted color provides. If you convert an image to CMYK using a heavy black, then black takes over the function of the unwanted color and some of this loss can be avoided.*

Images whose main subjects (or color casts) are predominantly red, green, or blue are prime candidates for adjustments to the unwanted color channel—red is the complement of cyan, green is the complement of magenta, and blue is the complement of yellow. Problems with nonprimary colors or with two dominant image colors are a bit trickier, but only because you need to think in terms of two complementary colors rather than one. You've seen several examples in this chapter that put this theory nicely into practice.

Matching Colors

Exact color matching is a daily routine for print professionals who produce documents for marketing and advertising purposes. This is one field to which the rule about not making local selections to "fix" color problems doesn't necessarily apply. It's always good to begin by adjusting color for the entire image, but if you suddenly have to change the color of a clothing item because the manufacturer ran out of stock on the first color, then nothing but a local selection will do.

A good basic strategy for exact color matching is to calibrate your monitor on a daily or weekly basis, to prepare contract proofs of critical product-color images, and to match those proofs to both the original product and the monitor before sending the document out to print. A colorimetric device such as the Colortron from Light Source Computing, which can match spectrometric color data across different media, can be invaluable for this type of work (see Chapter 4). Careful attention to ambient lighting is vital, since you should ideally match product colors under the lighting conditions in which the intended customer will view them.

HLS-type adjustments are especially intuitive for color-matching work. Changing the hue, saturation, or lightness values of a selected product using tools such as Photoshop's Hue/Saturation or Selective Color options often works more quickly and efficiently than whole-image curve adjustments.

If there's any message that we hope we've conveyed clearly in this chapter, it's that there are usually several techniques from which you can choose when making color adjustments to an image. When deciding on the best strategy, be mindful of the relative importance of the subjects in each image. Make color adjustments that benefit detail, contouring, and liveliness in the subjects that are most essential—at the expense of less vital subjects, if that becomes necessary.

9

Resolution and Sizing for Print Media

Coordinating the resolution of an image with the physical size at which it will be output is one of the most important tasks in preparing an image for print. If the resolution is too low—that is, if the image contains too little data for the final output size—the printed version will not show enough detail and may even evidence "jaggies." There are also negative consequences if the resolution is much *higher* than necessary: workflow is needlessly bottlenecked, excessively large file sizes make output more expensive, and contrast relationships may become muddier. The ideal, of course, is to determine the optimum output size and resolution for every image in every print project. Helping you to achieve that goal is the subject of this chapter.

Types of Resolution

Before we can provide useful guidelines for determining optimum resolution, it's important to be clear about our terminology. This is no small feat for "resolution," a term that everyone throws around so loosely it seems to apply to everything and mean nothing at all. There's scanning resolution, optical resolution, image resolution, display resolution, output resolution, and printer resolution, just to name a few. What resolution means in a given context depends on the stage of the production process and the device that's doing the measuring.

When working in print media, your primary concern should be with three types of resolution: input resolution, output resolution, and printer resolution. We'll also cover a few other types of resolution that you should be familiar with.

Input Resolution

Input resolution measures the density of information that an input device captures per linear inch or centimeter when digitizing an image. When the input device is a flatbed, transparency, or drum scanner, input resolution is used interchangeably with *scanning resolution* and is measured in pixels per inch (ppi) or dots per inch (dpi). When the digitizing device is a digital camera, input resolution is measured in terms of the total number of pixels captured along the horizontal and vertical grid of the camera's CCD array. For example, the Nikon E2 has an input resolution of 1,280 × 1,000 pixels.

Most scanners and many digital cameras offer variable input resolutions. If you know the final print dimensions and the halftone screen frequency at the time you first capture an image, you can select a scanning or input resolution that yields the exact amount of information necessary for output. This is desirable because you can thereby avoid having to add information to or subtract information from the image at a later time, which could negatively impact print quality. The "How Much Data Do You Need?" section of this chapter contains a limited number of formulas for determining the best input resolution for an image based on other print-related parameters.

Output Resolution

Input resolution has nothing to do with *output resolution*—the density of information required for final output to a color printer, imagesetter, platesetter, or digital press. The output resolution for a given project is determined by a combination of printer resolution and halftone screen frequency (unless you're using FM screening) and should be the same for all images in a document. So even though the source images for a print project may be digitized at many different resolutions using a variety of input devices, they all need to be at a common output resolution before final output. To get them there, you may need to change the resolution of an image (which affects its size), the amount of information it contains, or both.

Output resolution is a major determinant of print quality (Figure 9–1). An output resolution far lower than what the print vendor recommends can cause a printed image to lack detail and look grainy. On the other hand, an excessively high output resolution increases output time and costs unnecessarily and can result in a subtle loss of contrast.

Note: *Experts disagree about the ideal relationship between output resolution and halftone screen frequency, but for most applications, a ratio of 1.5:1 works well and yields excellent contrast and detail (see Chapter 3).*

Printer Resolution

Printer resolution, sometimes called *output device resolution*, refers to the number of dots per inch that a printer, imagesetter, or platesetter generates during output. When the final output device is a continuous-tone printer, near-realistic image reproduction is possible as long as the output resolution is roughly equal to the printer resolution. But with halftoning devices such as laser printers, imagesetters, and plate-

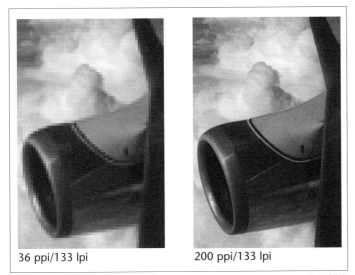

| 36 ppi/133 lpi | 200 ppi/133 lpi |

© Emil Ihrig

Figure 9–1

*Output resolution can contribute to or detract from the printed quality of an image. **Left:** Extremely low output resolution causes an image to appear grainy or pixelated. **Right:** Correct output resolution yields an eye-pleasing balance between contrast and detail.*

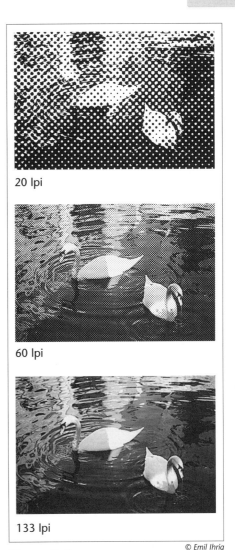

20 lpi

60 lpi

133 lpi

© Emil Ihrig

Figure 9–2

Halftone screen frequency controls the level of detail in a printed image. All images in these examples have been output at 2,540 dpi, which permits reproduction of a full range of tones at all of the screen frequencies shown above.

setters, printer resolution and halftone screen frequency are equally important in determining whether a photographic image can preserve the appearance of continuous tone when printed. As Figure 9–2 shows, halftone screen frequency controls the level of detail that can be reproduced in a printed image, but it's the relationship *between* screen frequency and printer resolution that controls the smoothness of transitions between adjacent tones. For truly smooth transitions, an output device that uses halftoning must be able to reproduce 256 tones per ink color at the screen frequency used. That's simply not possible at printer resolutions of 300 or 600 dpi. Even when printing at 1,200 dpi, you can achieve 256-tone output only at screen frequencies of 75 lpi or lower, which are suitable for newsprint applications only. At printer resolutions of 2,400, it's possible to reproduce a full tonal range at any screen frequency up to 150 lpi, and output devices with even greater resolution capabilities can reproduce full tonal ranges at still higher screen frequencies. (Table 9–1 in the "How Much Data Do You Need?" section of this chapter includes formulas to help you calculate the maximum number of tones per color that can be reproduced at a given halftone screen frequency.)

Other Faces of Resolution

If you're clear about the distinctions between input resolution, output resolution, and printer resolution and their respective roles in print reproduction, you need have only a nodding acquaintance with the other types of resolution you're likely to encounter: optical and interpolated resolution, image resolution, and display resolution.

Optical Resolution and Interpolated Resolution

Manufacturers of desktop flatbed and transparency scanners quote input resolution in two different ways. A scanner's *optical resolution* indicates the highest input resolution of which its optical system is capable. However, advertisements for desktop scanners usually cite the equipment's maximum *interpolated* resolution, which is often two to four times higher. At interpolated resolutions, a scanner isn't capturing additional "real" data; instead, it's creating new pixels between the pixels its optical system can sample, based on educated digital guesses about what tonal values to plug in between adjacent pixels. To maximize input quality, avoid scanning at resolutions higher than the maximum optical resolution whenever possible (see Figure 9–3).

Tip: *Applying an unsharp masking filter to an image that has been scanned using interpolation doesn't add new detail, but it mitigates some of the apparent fuzziness.*

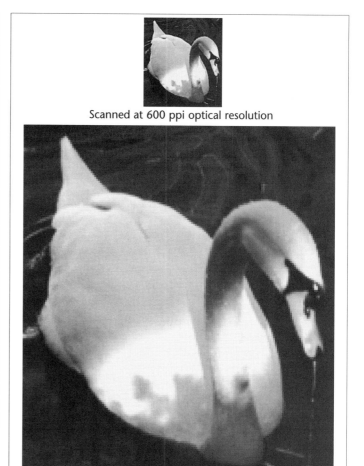

Scanned at 600 ppi optical resolution

Scanned at 2,400 ppi interpolated resolution

Figure 9–3   © Emil Ihrig

Scanning at interpolated resolutions affects image quality adversely. **Top:** *An extract from an image captured at a flatbed scanner's maximum optical resolution of 600 ppi.* **Bottom:** *The same sample captured at an interpolated resolution of 2,400 ppi contains many more pixels but no more "true" detail, so a close-up reveals fuzziness.*

Image Resolution

Image resolution is another term used to imply far too many things. In its purest sense, it indicates the horizontal and vertical dimensions of a digital image expressed in pixels—4,000 × 2,666 pixels, for instance. Digital cameras and film/transparency scanners express the fixed amount of information they can capture in terms of image resolution, and film recorders express the fixed image sizes they can output in the same way.

Note: *What resolution specifications for film recorders actually communicate is only a pixel stream, not actual resolving power—the maximum number of line pairs per millimeter that film recorders can record. For example, an 8,000-line film recorder can't really place a series of distinct 1/8,000-inch marks on a piece of film. The pixels overlap each other, softening or obliterating detail that may have existed in the high-definition original.*

Display Resolution

Monitor resolution or *display resolution* has two different meanings in popular usage. In one sense, it describes the number of pixels that a monitor can display horizontally and vertically at one time. The higher a monitor's display resolution, the more you can see of an image at one time as you work. If your chief activity is page layout, a monitor resolution of $1,152 \times 870$ or greater is advisable. For dedicated image-editing professionals who routinely work with large-scale, high-resolution images, it may pay to use a monitor that's capable of even higher display resolutions, such as $1,600 \times 1,200$.

The second usage describes the number of dots or pixels per inch on the screen. There's a wide variance here among manufacturers and models. Dedicated Macintosh monitors have a standardized display resolution of 72 dpi, which at a 1:1 viewing magnification provides realistic measurements for page layout professionals. Nonstandardized PC monitors have display resolutions ranging from 72 dpi to more than 100 dpi.

Note: *Monitor resolution is almost always lower than the output resolution you assign to images. Images therefore tend to appear much larger on the screen than they do in print.*

How Much Data Do You Need?

There's more to determining resolution and sizing for an image than just setting an output resolution. The crucial question is how much *data* an image should contain to ensure that it will reproduce well in print. This question can take many forms, depending on what information has already been supplied by an art director or print vendor and what is still unknown. What's the largest output size you can assign without having to add more data to an image through resampling? What's the highest screen frequency you can use and still retain detail and smooth tonal transitions? What minimum imagesetter or platesetter resolution is required to support your planned screen frequency?

Arriving at the answers to these and other data-related output questions is like filling in the missing pieces of a jigsaw puzzle. The pieces you already have in place can help you fit the remaining pieces together. In the same way, if you know a few of the parameters listed here, you can use the formulas in Table 9–1 to determine the information that's still missing:

- Print dimensions (the size at which the image will be printed in the final document)
- Vertical and horizontal image resolution (in pixels)
- Output resolution
- Printer resolution
- Halftone screen frequency (assuming use of a conventional AM screening technology)

To Determine. . .	If You Already Know. . .	Use This Formula:
Output resolution, optimum for halftoning device output	Screen frequency	Screen frequency x 1.5
Output resolution, optimum for continuous-tone device output	Printer resolution	Printer resolution x 1
Maximum print dimensions, halftoned output	Number of pixels along horizontal or vertical dimension (depending on which dimension is critical for layout purposes) Screen frequency	Number of pixels ÷ (Screen frequency x 1.5)
Maximum print dimensions, continuous-tone output	Number of pixels along horizontal or vertical dimension (depending on which dimension is critical for layout purposes) Printer resolution	Number of pixels ÷ Printer resolution
Maximum tones per ink color, halftoned output	Printer resolution Screen frequency	(Printer resolution ÷ Screen frequency)^2 + 1
Minimum printer resolution required for smooth tonal transitions, halftoned output	Screen frequency	Screen frequency x 16
Maximum screen frequency permitted to retain smooth tonal transitions, halftoned output	Printer resolution	Printer resolution ÷ 16
Image resolution (one dimension), required to output at desired print dimensions without resampling, in pixels (halftoned output)	Print dimension Screen frequency	Print dimension x (Screen frequency x 1.5)
Image resolution in pixels (one dimension), required to output at desired print dimensions without resampling (continuous-tone or FM-screened output)	Print dimension Output resolution	Print dimension x Output resolution

Table 9–1

Calculating Output Resolution, Print Dimensions, Tonal Range Reproduction, Printer Resolution, Screen Frequency, and Image Resolution

Tip: *Don't choose a screen frequency arbitrarily. Paper stock and press setup considerations determine the maximum screen frequency that can hold a halftone dot successfully. Obtain the advice of your print vendor and service bureau or color house.*

Output Resolution and the "Halftoning Factor"

You may recall from Chapter 3 that the screening technology used to output an image impacts the amount of data the image file should contain. Halftoning (still the mainstream technology) involves the use of screen angles, the mathematics of which suggest that the ideal relationship between output resolution and screen frequency should be approximately 1.5:1. For an assigned screen frequency of 150 lpi, for example, an output resolution of 225 ppi is usually sufficient to deliver high-quality reproduction.

Some prepress vendors at the high end of the market dispute the 1.5:1 theory, preferring a resolution-to-screen frequency ratio of 2:1. According to these professionals, a screen frequency of 150 demands an output resolution of 300 ppi in order to ensure quality. Current trends favor the 1.5:1 ratio (which also leads to much smaller file sizes), but take the advice of the professionals you trust most and who have a history of performing for you.

Output Resolution for Continuous-Tone Printers

When the final output device is a continuous-tone printer such as a dye sublimation printer, or an output device that simulates continuous tone (a color photocopier or an inkjet printer), the printer resolution itself is the deciding factor. An output resolution equal to the printer resolution—say, 300 ppi for a 300-dpi dye sublimation printer—gives good results. If your final output device will be an imagesetter or platesetter, save two versions of the image: one that exactly matches the output resolution of the proofing device and one that contains the correct resolution for the final output device.

Output Resolution for FM Screening

The FM and stochastic screening technologies first discussed in Chapter 3 do away with regular halftone screening patterns, but they still use PostScript halftoning devices for final output. Some FM-screening software solutions still offer a nominal screen frequency, while others correlate FM dot sizes with the size of the smallest halftone dot that the final output device can reproduce at the nominal frequency.

To determine the best output resolution to use with FM screening, ask yourself whether you will be satisfied with output quality comparable to what you would obtain with digital halftoning, or whether you want to aim for something even better. If you merely want to match the output quality of halftone screening, you can get good results with a quality ratio of 1:1, which results in very small file sizes. For example, you can use 150 ppi output resolution when the equivalent screen frequency would be 150 lpi. But if you will be printing on high-quality coated stock, if you can use a high total ink coverage, or if you will be using HiFi color, you should assign higher output resolutions (up to 300 ppi), to take full advantage of FM screening's superior ability to reproduce detail.

Output Resolution for Bitmaps

Bitmaps, which consist of strictly black-and-white pixels, have rules of their own when it comes to output resolution, whether they're produced using halftoning, continuous-tone devices, or FM screening. Use an output resolution that's equal to the printer resolution of the final output device or 1,200 ppi, whichever is lower. A bitmap to be output on a 600 dpi printer, for example, should also be at a 600-ppi resolution; when output to a 2,400-dpi imagesetter, the same bitmap yields the best definition at 1,200 dpi. Setting the resolution higher than 1,200 seems to make no visible difference; in fact, many viewers have a hard time distinguishing any improvement in reproduction characteristics above 600 ppi (see Figure 9–4 for a comparison of several different bitmap resolutions, all output to the same device at 2,540 dpi). Output

150 ppi

300 ppi

600 ppi

1,200 ppi

Figure 9–4

The detail in black-and-white line art reproduces most smoothly when the output resolution of the image equals the resolution of the final output device, up to a maximum of 1,200 ppi.

resolutions of 600 to 1,200 ppi may sound high when you're accustomed to working with continuous-tone images, but remember that file sizes for bitmaps are 24 times smaller than for color images of comparable dimensions.

Resizing and Resampling Images

The reality of day-to-day print production dictates that different people are usually responsible for the processes of input, prepress preparation, and output. Even when one person controls most of these processes, plans for sizing or output can change. One result is that many of the digital images you receive have been input at a size and resolution other than what's required for final output. Altering the size, resolution, or amount of information in an image is, therefore, one of the essential prepress tasks you must handle.

When and how you adapt sizing and resolution affects the integrity and quality of the final printed image. What's the difference between adjusting size or resolution only and altering the amount of data in the image? At what point in the production process should changes to sizing and/or resolution take place? And how should you handle such changes for an image that's likely to be used for multiple projects—perhaps even for other forms of output besides print? Let's establish some ground rules.

Sizing Strategies

There are basically only three scenarios that call for adjustments to the physical size and/or output resolution of an image:

- Adjusting physical size and output resolution without altering the amount of data in a file

- Decreasing the amount of data in a file in order to reduce image size and/or output resolution

- Increasing the amount of data in the file in order to enlarge image size and/or increase output resolution

The first alternative is always preferable if the file contains the right amount of data to support the required size and output resolution. If the file contains too much or too little data, one of the other steps becomes necessary.

Caution: *When resizing an image or changing its resolution, always remember to maintain the current aspect ratio. Otherwise, the resulting image will be distorted.*

Strategy 1: Adjusting Size and Resolution While Maintaining File Size

Every production professional's dream is that the original scanned or digitally captured file will contain just the right amount of data for output so that its quality won't have to be compromised by adding or subtracting information. When this is the case, the original resolution may be too high for output and the physical output size too small, or vice versa, but you can adjust these without increasing or decreasing the amount of information in the file.

Most image sizing dialog boxes like the one shown in Figure 9–5 give you the option of constraining file size. When file size is constrained,

© Emil Ihrig

Figure 9–5

Maintaining a constant file size causes the physical dimensions of an image to change when you change the resolution, and vice versa, much like the reciprocal action of a see-saw. Here, the original scan is 7.94 x 5.38 picas at 1,012 ppi but it becomes larger in size (40.17 x 27.21 picas) when output resolution is decreased to 200 ppi. Image quality is not affected because the total amount of data remains the same.

there's a reciprocal relationship between resolution and the physical size of the picture; increasing the output resolution reduces output size, while decreasing the resolution increases output size. There's no potentially adverse impact on image quality, though, because the amount of data in the image remains constant.

Strategy 2: Downsampling

If you can't anticipate final output size and resolution at the time of scanning or capture, it's better to include excess data in the file than not to include enough. You can eliminate the excess data later when you're preparing for final output. Decreasing the amount of information in a file by reducing the dimensions, the resolution, or both, is called *downsampling*. There's always a quality loss when you change the amount of information in a file after the first save, but the eye doesn't perceive the loss when you *decrease* the amount of data, because you're only throwing out information that the final output device can't use anyway. That's especially the case with PostScript-based halftoning devices, which use an averaging process during output and jettison any excess pixels. With FM-screened output, it's even more important not to include more pixels for final output than necessary, since the additional information translates to increased dot density and possibly to an unwelcome increase in dot gain.

To downsample a file, make certain that the file size is *not* constrained, and then alter the dimensions or resolution as necessary.

Strategy 3: Interpolation (Upsampling)

Adding data to an image file is the least desirable alternative, because interpolation adds no "real" detail and results in a softer-looking image. If an image doesn't contain enough information to reproduce well at the desired output size and resolution, it's preferable to rescan or recapture it a second time. But if that isn't an option—for example, if the image came from an outside source who can't or won't supply a replacement—then *upsampling* through interpolation is your only choice.

Tip: Many imaging professionals maintain that if the original scan contains plenty of detail, interpolation has no visible effect on image quality. Content and viewing distance are the important factors.

To upsample an image, make certain that the file size is *not* constrained, and then alter the dimensions and/or resolution as necessary. Some image-editing packages offer a choice of interpolation methods; Adobe Photoshop, for example, provides Nearest Neighbor, Bilinear, and Bicubic options. In general, the speedier the interpolation method, the lower the quality of the results; but there are exceptions to this rule. If you want an image to have a slightly jagged, "techie" look, then a high-speed method akin to Nearest Neighbor might be just what you're looking for. Bilinear interpolation, a medium-speed method that tends to blur and soften detail, can be the technique of choice when the original image contains unsightly artifacts that you'd rather tone down. Bicubic interpolation is preferable when you want to preserve every detail, warts and all, with as little quality loss as possible.

Size Before You Sharpen

Fix the output size and output resolution of an image only after the layout is final *and* a prepress or print vendor has given you all the necessary information concerning output device resolution, screening technology, and screen frequency (if applicable). If you downsize an image as soon as you know the final layout size but before you have exact output specifications, you might inadvertently jettison data that you'll need if the screen frequency is higher than you anticipated. By the same token, avoid adding data to an image through interpolation before you have output specifications in hand; you might be adding pixels that you don't really need, at the expense of image quality.

Tip: *If you don't receive output specifications until the last minute, resize images to fit the layout but without changing the amount of information in the image. Then make final resampling adjustments just prior to output.*

Sizing and resolution changes can take place before or after you perform tonal and color correction, but you should definitely make them *before* you sharpen. That's because larger, higher-resolution images can handle more sharpening than smaller, less dense ones. If you sharpen a large image optimally and then downsample it to a much smaller size or lower resolution, the final printed version might contain visible artifacts. Similarly, sharpening a low-resolution or small image and then upsampling it to a larger size and/or higher resolution can result in a picture that looks soft.

Multiple-Use Images

These days, digital images can easily undergo several uses for different projects—appearing once as a full-page color magazine advertise-

ment, two or three times as a small, black-and-white newspaper ad, again on a company video, and yet another time on a promotional or educational CD-ROM. If you suspect that an image is destined for such multipurposing (even if you've made no concrete plans), follow this strategy before altering size or resolution for your print project:

1. Scan or capture the original at the largest size possible, commensurate with the most data-intensive use the image is likely to see. Large-scale color print reproductions entail the largest file sizes and highest output resolutions.

2. Duplicate the original file. Archive the original for future use and save the duplicate under a new name for your print project.

3. Adapt the size and resolution of the duplicate file as necessary.

This same strategy applies to other prepress processes such as sharpening and color correction, too.

In this chapter, we've demystified the concepts behind resolution; clarified its importance in the production process; and covered the when, why, and how of adjusting it. In Chapter 10, we'll address the important issue of sharpening and other special-case adjustments that must sometimes be made to improve output quality.

10

Sharpening and Special-Case Adjustments

You've retouched and color separated every image in your document to perfection, tweaked ink balance, adjusted highlights and shadows, compensated for dot gain, and determined the perfect settings for halftone or FM screening. What's left? In this chapter, we help you tidy up any remaining loose ends in the prepress production of images. We'll survey strategies for sharpening, for making special-case adjustments such as the removal of noise or screening, and for trapping color images. We'll also discuss important prepress considerations for choosing an appropriate file format.

Sharpening Strategies

Sharpening is an important step for all images that have a printed document as their final destination, for exactly two reasons: input and output.

- **Input**—Scanned images and Photo CD images always need sharpening, because the scanning process itself introduces a certain amount of fuzziness. (For a better understanding of this phenomenon, see our companion book, *Scanning the Professional Way*.) Captures from digital cameras usually need sharpening, too, because the CCD elements in all but the most high-end cameras are prone to the same types of noise problems as the CCDs in desktop scanners. Only drum scanners and sophisticated midrange desktop scanners can attack this input-related lack of sharpness on the fly, even before the first save.

■ **Output**—The printing process also tends to soften the look of images, due primarily to the vagaries of paper-and-ink interaction. In consequence, you should always sharpen images a little more than you think you need to, because the end product will always look slightly softer on paper than it does on your monitor.

Digital sharpening is *not* a fix for poor camera work; it can't create crisp clarity from an out-of-focus original. What good sharpening techniques *can* do is increase contrast in an image in a way that enhances the perception of contours. There's more than one technique for sharpening an image, and not all are equally effective.

Simple Contrast-Enhancing Techniques

The most basic techniques for sharpening an image involve simply enhancing contrast, either globally through the use of brightness and contrast adjustments or sharpening filters, or locally through the use of sharpening tools. When applied globally, contrast enhancement is a sledgehammer approach to sharpening; it wipes out subtle detail as it pushes image data toward the tonal extremes. To produce selective crispness in an image, you need more refined techniques. But there are circumstances in which high-contrast, low-detail images may be exactly what you need—for example, when a low-budget publication will be printed on highly absorbent stock that can't reproduce a broad range of tones.

Enhancing contrast in limited areas of an image, on the other hand, can greatly improve the perception of sharpness overall. The key is to increase contrast in the most important subjects, in lighter tonal ranges such as the quartertones, and in the areas to which the eye immediately travels.

Edge-Sharpening and Noise Filters

When you want more control over sharpening than contrast enhancement affords but you don't have access to a good unsharp masking filter, edge-sharpening or noise filters can sometimes do the job. *Edge-sharpening filters* sharpen selectively, increasing contrast only where clear transitions in tonal values already exist. The end result is that existing contours are accentuated, while areas that contain low-contrast, subtle detail are left unaltered. Some edge-sharpening filters give you additional control by allowing you to specify just how much of a difference in tonal range must exist between adjacent pixels before the filter kicks in.

Noise filters increase contrast by introducing pixels of random tonal value, thus creating a perception of improved sharpness. They're most useful when you apply them to limited areas of an image that are especially flat. Avoid applying high amounts of noise to an entire image, unless you want a grainy look. Monochrome noise is more effective than multicolored noise for sharpening purposes.

Tip: To avoid banding in images that contain gradients (especially gradients with gradual rather than high-contrast transitions), apply small amounts of noise to the gradient areas.

Unsharp Masking (USM) Filters

Unsharp masking (USM), the most sophisticated type of sharpening technique, has its origins in the not-so-long-ago days of traditional press-work. Camera operators in the stripping department would enhance sharpness by creating a mask that exaggerated contrast along edges, shooting a blurry version of the same image and then photographically blending the two versions. The result was to increase edge sharpness without creating an artificial look and without eliminating detail in areas of low contrast. Digital unsharp masking filters perform an equivalent task, generating a blurred version of the original on the fly as pixel-by-pixel comparison takes place. (That's one reason why USM filters are so slow.)

Most incarnations of USM offer tremendous control over the sharpening process, but you must define settings intelligently. The most well-known example of a USM filter, Adobe Photoshop's Unsharp Mask (Figure 10–1), lets you determine three significant parameters: what constitutes an edge, the degree of contrast enhancement along edges, and the width of the path along which edge comparisons and sharpening occur. Here's how each parameter affects sharpening:

- **Amount**—This setting determines the degree of the contrast enhancement that takes place along edges. 100 percent doubles the existing sharpness, 200 percent doubles it again, and so on.

- **Radius**—When the filter detects an edge, the Radius setting determines how wide a path (in tenths of a pixel) will be used for tone comparison and contrast enhancement. The Radius setting is especially critical; if the path is too wide, the result is a *halo effect,* where edges are surrounded by visible outlines of extreme opposite contrast and color (Figure 10–2). A rule of thumb for deriving

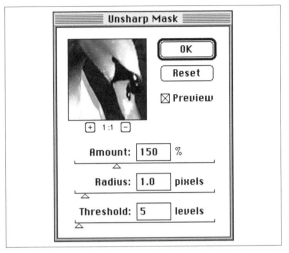

Figure 10–1

The options in Photoshop's Unsharp Mask dialog box let you define how much sharpening occurs, where it occurs, and what constitutes an edge.

the appropriate Radius setting is to divide the output resolution by 200. With an output resolution of 200 ppi, for example, a Radius of approximately 1.0 pixels should yield good results.

- **Threshold**—This setting defines the minimum difference in tonal value between adjacent pixels that must exist in order for an edge to be present. With a setting of zero, contrast among *all* pixels is exaggerated, which defeats the subtlety of which USM is capable. Typically, you can get good results using values between 2 and 6 (see the guidelines that follow).

Guidelines for Unsharp Masking

Here are some basic navigational instructions to help you determine optimum USM settings for your own images:

- Sharpen images only *after* you have sampled them to the correct, final output size and resolution. Optimum settings for sharpening

Original scan, unsharpened

Appropriate USM settings

Excessive USM applied

Figure 10–2

© *Emil Ihrig*

Applying USM with appropriate Amount, Radius, and Threshold settings is the key to obtaining eye-pleasing sharpness, with subtle tonal gradations maintained and without haloing. **Top:** *Before USM, this image looks slightly milky in print.* **Center:** *This version is sharpened appropriately for the subject matter, the size, and the output resolution (200 ppi).* **Bottom:** *Applying unsharp masking with too broad a radius can result in visible haloing, when tonal contrast is pushed to unrealistic extremes. Notice the great reduction in tonal gradation and detail.*

are resolution and size dependent; so if you sharpen first and then resize drastically, the printed version could look fuzzier (if enlarged or upsampled) or more artificially high in contrast (if reduced or downsampled) than it should.

- Whenever possible, set output highlight and shadow points *after* sharpening (see Chapter 7). Sharpening pushes contrast beyond current limits and can introduce unwanted speculars or loss of detail in the shadows if you've set the boundaries of the tonal range previously.

- Originals that are already in good focus do well with USM amounts at or near 100 percent. Reserve higher settings for high-resolution images that will be printed at large sizes, poorly scanned originals, or images that will be printed on absorbent paper stocks and that can therefore benefit from higher contrast levels.

- Images that feature close-ups (especially of human subjects) require less sharpening than other types of images. To avoid mottled complexions or accentuation of cosmetic defects, keep Threshold settings high (4 to 6) and Radius settings low. Figure 10–3 compares USM settings for two images of equal size—one a facial close-up, the other a medium-range outdoor scene containing many small details.

Note: *Captures from digital cameras that store images in JPEG format ideally should be sharpened before the first save. Post-JPEG sharpening exaggerates the edges of the 8 × 8 pixel blocks that JPEG processing creates. If presave sharpening isn't possible, use subtle unsharp masking parameters—particularly a low radius and a high threshold setting.*

Figure 10–3   © Emil Ihrig

*Radius settings should be low and Threshold settings high for close-ups, especially close-ups of faces or people (**top**). Medium-range or panoramic subjects containing many small details, on the other hand, benefit from higher Radius and lower Threshold settings (**bottom**).*

- To reduce the risk of haloing, keep Radius near 1.0 pixels, especially on low-resolution images or images that will be printed at small sizes. High-resolution images that will be printed at large sizes often can tolerate slightly higher values.

- Images 15MB and larger often can tolerate sharpening amounts between 250 and 500 percent. For very small images, keep Radius settings at 0.5 pixels or lower.

Sharpening the Black Channel Only

Many of the significant contours and edges in CMYK images appear in the black channel (see Chapter 6). For this reason, you often can make a color image look crisper by sharpening the black channel alone. This strategy avoids the risk of unanticipated color shifts that you incur when you tweak contrast in all four color channels at once. It also allows you to sharpen somewhat more heavily than usual, with fewer consequences. Try darkening the black quarter-tone slightly; the eye is especially sensitive to this part of the tonal range and will perceive stronger quartertone contours as sharper.

Sharpening in LAB Color

Whether you're starting with an RGB or a CMYK original, a useful sharpening strategy is to convert the image to LAB color temporarily, strengthen contrast and detail in the Luminance channel, and then reconvert. In LAB mode, the Luminance channel controls contrast and light-to-dark relationships independent of color content, so sharpening is intuitive—a matter of adjusting curves as though you were performing color correction in some more familiar color mode. (Don't casually try color correction in LAB's A and B channels, though; it's definitely *not* intuitive.) A careful sharpening of the Luminance channel that strengthens contrast at strategic tonal junctures can often do the trick, as Figure 10–4 and Figure C–22 in the Color Gallery demonstrate.

Tip: *The benefits you derive from converting a CMYK image to LAB mode and sharpening it there depend in part on the color separation settings in effect when you reconvert the image back to CMYK. Be sure that you don't get more or less black than you intended; review Chapter 6 for assistance.*

Figure 10–4

© Emil Ihrig

*The Luminance channel in LAB color mode contains the contrast information for an image. Sharpening this one channel and then reconverting the image to CMYK often results in a perceived improvement in sharpness. **Left to right:** The Luminance channel for the original image in Figure C-22 in the Color Gallery, the USM settings for the Luminance channel, and the sharpened Luminance channel for the final version of Figure C–22.*

Toward "Sharper" Color

In a color image, it's impossible to totally separate contrast from color, because changes to brightness levels inevitably cause some slight color shifting. The trick is to arrange the shifts in such a way that the viewer perceives only heightened resolving power and detail. A corollary principle is that if you correct and enhance color satisfactorily, images automatically will *appear* to be sharper than they originally were. So if an image looks fuzzy, sharpening may not solve the problem; you may need to clean up the color using curve adjustments instead. See Chapter 8 for examples of how channel-by-channel curve adjustments and channel blending operations can improve perceived definition in an image even as they cleanse dirty colors, control brilliance, manipulate saturation, and strengthen apparent contrast and detail. The problems that require correction in images can have many different causes—poor raw definition, poor color relationships, or poor density relationships, to name a few. Beware of lumping them all together conceptually and looking for a single, magic "one-size-fits-all" solution.

Descreening Previously Printed Images

In cases of historical photographs or where an undigitized original has inadvertently been lost or destroyed, it's sometimes necessary to scan and reprint images that have been printed previously. (If you make a habit of doing this for other reasons, you may be violating copyright laws.) Since such images already have halftone screening embedded in them, reprinting them without first removing the previous screening can result in unsightly, grid-like moiré patterning caused by overlapping screens of different angles (see Figure 10–5). You can attack and conquer this potential problem in one of several ways:

■ *Descreen on the fly during scanning.* Drum scanners and an increasing number of desktop flatbed and slide scanners include a descreening filter that lets you remove previous halftone patterning automatically. The only catch, at least with lower-end scanners, is that you usually have to specify the original halftone screen frequency in order for the job to be done correctly. If you don't know and can't determine the exact halftone screen frequency of the original print job, you're in for some trial and error.

■ *Descreen as a postprocessing operation.* For do-it-yourselfers, the object is to first blur the embedded halftone patterning and then restore as much contrast and detail as possible without making the old patterning visible again. Scan the previously printed original at a resolution that's slightly higher than the frequency of the embedded halftone screening—if the original appears to have been halftoned at 133 lpi, for example,

scan it at 150 lpi. (You can usually estimate the original frequency closely by eyeballing the original with a loupe and observing the quality of the paper on which it was printed.) Then, in an image-editing package, apply a Blur, Median, or Gaussian Blur filter at a low setting, followed by a moderate application of an unsharp masking filter.

No descreening applied

Descreening applied

Figure 10–5

Previously printed scanned images can show moiré patterning if you print them a second time without first removing the existing screening.

Preventing Content Moiré

Fabric samples and other images that contain regular patterns also run the risk of printing with moiré, if a conflict between the content and the designated halftone screen frequency generates interference patterns. To help avoid this potential problem, try the following preventive measures:

- *Use FM screening rather than halftone (AM) screening.* Since FM screening technologies don't produce regular patterning, there's no opportunity for moiré to raise its ugly head (see Chapter 3). As a tradeoff, you'll have to wrestle with higher amounts of dot gain. Software developers are continuing to produce improved solutions to this problem.

- *Add noise to the patterned area or blur it slightly.* Noise, especially monochromatic noise, tones down edges and patterning and makes them less obvious. Alternatively, as with previously screened originals, you can use a Median or Gaussian Blur filter to smooth the edges of the patterning and then sharpen edges to reintroduce some of the contrast lost.

- *Switch color plate angles.* With the help of your print vendor, determine which color plate is most likely to cause interference with the content patterning, and swap its screen angle with that of another plate that's less likely to offend.

- *Print the image at a size that won't interfere with halftone patterning.* If possible, choose an output size for which the repeating content patterns won't conflict with the halftone screening. Measure the size of the content "tiles" and then adjust image size so that the screen frequency is evenly divisible by neither the width nor the height of each tile.

Trapping Raster Images

Printing is an art, not a science, no matter how technologically sophisticated the tools have become. Many mechanical, environmental, and human factors beyond a designer's control can bring about a less-than-perfect alignment of color plates on press. That's why *trapping*—the process of intentionally overlapping adjoining colors in electronic artwork and document files—is important wherever solid colors in a document or in an artwork file abut one another. Without trapping, misregistration can cause unsightly gaps between colors to appear in the final printed document.

Continuous-tone images rarely require trapping, simply because color distribution is so random that they typically have no large areas of solid color abutting against other solid colors. There are exceptions, of course. Fashion shots and close-ups of single subjects sometimes contain these types of color junctures, but the most common instance you need to be concerned with is vector images.

"Vector images?" you ask. "Isn't this a book about prepress for *raster* images?" Yes, but any seasoned print publications professional knows that many PostScript vector drawings are so complex and contain so many nodes that they easily choke any imagesetter or platesetter. One of the safest (though memory-hogging!) ways to circumvent such troubles is to rasterize vector files in Adobe Photoshop (or Adobe Illustrator 6 or later) at final output size and then place them in the layout. *Voilà*—a vector image has become a raster image, and you can tweak its color and tone exactly as you would any digital photograph. Right?

Not quite. Vector images typically consist of many solid-color elements, which means that they need to be trapped if you want to avoid the color gaps we've just described. You can trap them in the original vector drawing program, of course; but with the exception of Macromedia FreeHand (which features automatic trapping), you'll need to trap each object manually—a tedious task, and one that requires a high level of color skill. If your service bureau, color prepress vendor, or print vendor uses high-level trapping software such as Luminous TrapWise, you can avoid the trapping headaches altogether and just pay a third party to do the dirty work. But if you're on your own, a convenient solution is to trap rasterized vector images automatically in Photoshop, which precompensates for misregistration by making the trap color between any two abutting colors equal to the total of their color values. You can define trap amounts in terms of pixels, fractional points, or millimeters.

Determining the correct amount to trap for a given print project depends on the type of press, the halftone screen frequency (if you're using halftone screening), and the characteristics of the chosen paper stock. Your print vendor is the best resource for this information; but if you're unable to get reliable first-hand data, Table 10–1 offers a concise overview of recommended trap amounts that should at least get you in the ballpark.

Tip: *A quick way to calculate the appropriate trap amount for a project is to divide the size of each halftone dot by two. With a 150-line screen, for example, each halftone dot is 1 ÷ 150 = 0.00667 inches in diameter, which makes for a trap amount of .25 points (.0033 inches).*

Major page layout packages, notably QuarkXPress and Adobe PageMaker version 6 or later, provide automatic trapping for text and elements created within the page layout package itself. But no mainstream layout package currently traps imported images against native elements unless you use one of several third-party plug-in utilities available. The dos and don'ts of trapping elements created in a page layout program against imported images is a topic beyond the scope of this book. Suffice

Press Setup	Screen Frequency	Trap Amount (Points/Inches/mm)
Sheetfed, coated stock	150 lpi	.25/.003/.08
Sheetfed, uncoated stock	150 lpi	.25/.003/.08
Web offset, coated stock	150 lpi	.30/.004/.10
Web offset, uncoated stock	133 lpi	.40/.005/.13
Web offset, newsprint	85–100 lpi	.45/.006/.15
Flexographic, coated stock	133 lpi	.45/.006/.15
Flexographic, newsprint	85–100 lpi	.60/.008/.20
Flexographic, nonpaper substrates	65 lpi	.75/.010/.25
Rotogravure, coated stock	150 lpi	.25/.003/.08

Table 10–1
Recommended Trapping Values for Typical Press Setups

it to say that there are many tricky scenarios—gradients against solids and gradients against gradients being among the most nightmarish. If you must design documents with such complex color abutments, consider using a high-end PostScript trapping package or the services of a prepress vendor who has access to such a package.

Choosing a File Format

One of the more humdrum yet technically significant tasks you undertake when preparing an image for print is saving it in an appropriate file format. File formats differ greatly from one another in terms of the kinds of information they can store, but very few formats can save all the kinds of information necessary for high-quality, trouble-free PostScript print output. Over time, the two file formats that have proved themselves most durable for print publications are *TIFF* (*Tagged Image File Format*) and *EPS* (*Encapsulated PostScript*). Culprit formats to avoid include PICT, the nearly defunct PCX (once a mainstay of PC-platform graphics applications), and GIF, which is great for online file transfer but can't support the 16 million colors required for full-color print publications.

Flavors of TIFF

The TIFF file format, developed specifically for use in page-layout applications, is supported by all major image-editing, paint, and page-composition packages and is readable on multiple platforms. Several variants of TIFF exist; it's to your advantage to work with programs that support version 6.0 or later. The TIFF format offers the following advantages to print publications professionals:

- **Alpha channels**—TIFF files can save alpha channel information for applications that support it. Saving an image with alpha channels is handy when you need to continue editing local areas of an image between the time it's first placed in a page layout and the time you finally output it.

- **Compression**—With TIFF, you can compress files using lossless LZW (Lempel-Ziv-Welch) encoding, which typically reduces file size by about 50 percent. Most mainstream page composition packages support the import of LZW-compressed files.

- **Preseparations**—The TIFF format can save CMYK color separations within a single file, automatically generating color separations when you place the file in a page layout and output the document. The use of single-file separations reduces the risk of losing or misplacing files when you transfer them from one site to another.

On the downside, a CMYK TIFF file typically takes much longer to output than the same image saved in single-file DCS 2.0 EPS format (and somewhat longer than an image saved in five-file DCS 1.0 EPS format). The only type of duotone information a TIFF can save is a four-color process duotone (see Chapter 6).

EPS Files

The Encapsulated PostScript (abbreviated EPS or EPSF) file format is another cross-platform standard. Originally developed for the purpose of saving vector artwork in a way that allows users to place it within a page layout or another PostScript illustration, the EPS specification now includes raster artwork, too. As Figure 10–6 shows, the EPS format gives you more options and more control than any other file format. Its advantages for print media include these:

- **JPEG compression**—Unlike LZW TIFF compression, the JPEG standard allows you to

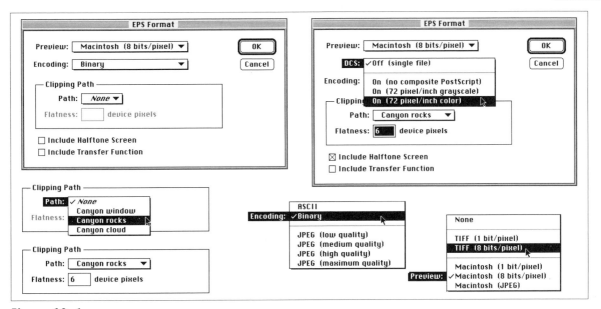

Figure 10–6

EPS Save options in Adobe Photoshop include choice of preview, preseparations, clipping paths, JPEG compression, and the option of embedding halftone screening and/or tone curve information.

reduce file size many times. JPEG compression is lossy compression, however, so the more heavily you compress a file, the greater the risk of image degradation. Many experts claim that a compression ratio of up to 10:1 yields excellent results without a visible loss in quality. With JPEG EPS files, you also need to consider platform- and application-related issues; not all page layout and illustration packages support importation of JPEG files, and many PC-based applications don't support it, either.

Note: *The color content of an image and the resolution at which it was originally digitized can help you predict just how much compression a given image can stand without incurring quality loss. If the details of interest are composed of blocks of solid color, you can use a fairly high compression ratio and still not notice much change, because color values in*

the image were similar to begin with. If an image is smoothly continuous in tone, on the other hand, a high compression ratio is likely to wipe out important gradations and result in a more visible loss of detail. Also, images digitized at a high resolution can stand more compression than images scanned at low resolution, because they contain a broader range of color values per linear unit of measurement. If an image contains finely detailed line artwork and text, avoid JPEGing it at all—the JPEG process will generate chromatic noise and other artifacts.

■ **Preseparations**—Thanks to the DCS (Desktop Color Separations) variant of the EPS file format, you can save color separations for a CMYK color image as either one file or as five files (one for each color plate, plus a user-definable preview). Some color prepress houses and service bureaus prefer the five-file DCS format over the single-file CMYK TIFF format because of the smaller preview files that DCS generates. Other vendors find that having to keep track of five files for every image makes customers more susceptible to file losses and resulting output delays.

- **Clipping paths**—By default, image files are always surrounded by a rectangular bounding box. If you want an irregular shape to print with a transparent background, you must create a *clipping path*—a mask around the irregular shape—in an image-editing program and then export the image as an EPS file. When you place the EPS file in a page layout or illustration, the background around the irregular shape drops out.

- **Duotones**—If you use Adobe Photoshop, you can save duotone information within the EPS file format (see Chapter 6).

- **Alpha channels**—Like TIFF, the EPS format can save alpha channel information.

- **Embedded halftone screening and tone curve information (transfer functions)**—Normally, all the images in a given page-layout document output with the same halftone screen settings. But if you want certain images to output differently from others in the document—say, at a lower screen frequency or at a different angle—you can embed that information directly in the EPS file. The image will then output at your custom settings, and no imagesetter operator will be able to alter them. The same is true for custom tone curves that you might want to apply to a given image within a document.

Caution: When you embed custom screening and transfer functions in an image, vendor personnel won't be able to troubleshoot your file or change settings should output problems arise.

Tip: Here's some in-the-trenches advice from experts. Use single-file DCS 2.0 when you trust the service provider and want to shorten output times considerably; TIFF when you're worried about losing track of files on a large job with a new service provider who may not have DCS 2.0 capability; and single-file DCS 1.0 when you're not concerned about output budget constraints.

Communicate, Communicate

In this age of information, nothing is more important than clear communication. For those of us in the print publishing field, that means finding out exactly what your service bureau, color prepress house, and print vendor expect from you at every stage in the production process and letting each of them know exactly what you want from them. The more you know about the parameters of your project, the better you can enhance your images and prepare each one for trouble-free, high-quality print output. Appendix A contains a handy list of technical questions that you can ask service and print vendors for each project. Bon voyage, and may you enjoy the journey!

Appendix A

An Image-Output Checklist

We believe heartily that the more responsibility you take for the technical preparation of your images, the more satisfied you will be with the final outcome. But the issues to consider in this field can be quite complex, so it's essential to know the right questions to ask. We've prepared a list of questions that you should fire at your partners in output at the start of every print project. Armed with the answers (and this book), you can expertly prep both color and black-and-white images for every type of print job.

Input Factors

- What are the sources of the images and how will they be or how were they digitized? What type of equipment or scanners are being used and what are their capabilities and limitations?

- What input resolution is recommended based on press setup and output parameters?

- What quality of originals are you being supplied with? If quality is under par, what do you have to do to bring them up to publication standards?

- Is color management being used to input originals? If so, what products are being used?

Press Setup

- What type of printing process will be used for the job—offset printing, flexography, rotogravure, etc.?

- If the job is specified for offset printing, what type of press will be used—web-fed, sheet-fed, or newspaper? What's the relative speed of the press and its consequences?

- What are the characteristics of the paper stock (or other substrate) on which the job will be printed? Is it coated or uncoated? What's the thickness? How absorbent is it? Are there any other characteristics that should be taken into consideration?

- What's the base color of the paper stock and how will it affect printed image color? What steps, if any, should be taken to compensate?

- What ink set will be used for the job? Are the inks wet or dry? If the job is process color, in what order will each color be laid down?

- Will files be output to paper, to film, direct to plate, or direct to press? (This factor has important ramifications for dot gain and registration.)

- Will final films/plates be positive or negative?

Specific Output Parameters

- What type of color proofing is adequate or recommended for this type of job— Chromalin, MatchPrint, Color Key, dye sublimation, and so on?

- What are the minimum and maximum dots that the press can hold for this job? (Take the answer with a grain of salt—print vendors tend to quote optimistically based on ideal conditions.)

- What is the maximum total ink coverage recommended for this job? What about black ink coverage?

- Should you use GCR or UCR separations? If GCR, should you also use UCA, and how much?

- If halftone screening is being specified for output, what screen frequency, angle, and dot shape are recommended?

- What's the approximate amount of dot gain that can be expected? Is dot gain being quoted in relative or absolute terms?

- Will FM screening be used? If so, how much dot gain should you compensate for?

- What output resolution do the service bureau, color house, and print vendor recommend for your images?

- What file format do the service bureau, color house, and print vendor prefer that you save images in?

- Do any of your images require trapping? Will the service bureau, color house, or print vendor provide automatic trapping? If not, what trapping amounts do you need to apply?

- Do any of your images have special characteristics (content patterns, line art, rasterized vector art, duotones, and so forth) that need to be considered in preparation for output? What measures are recommended?

- How many pages will be imposed on each plate? Can the print vendor provide a diagram of imposition page order to help designers place images, so that pages in which opposing color fields dominate don't end up immediately above and below each other on press? (If color problems occur in such situations, the opposing color content of adjacent pages makes color extremely difficult to correct; one page usually has to be sacrificed for the sake of the other.)

Index

Work Smart

Look Good

Subscribe To Color Publishing!

COLOR PUBLISHING

✂ *Please cut and return for processing*

YES! I want to work smart and look good with Color Publishing. Enter a 1-year (6 issues) subscription at the special low rate of $24.95—almost 20% off the cover price! I understand that if I am disappointed in any way, I may write "cancel" on the invoice, but keep my FREE issue.

❏ Payment enclosed   Charge My: ❏ American Express   ❏ Discover   ❏ MasterCard   ❏ EuroCard   ❏ VISA   ❏ Access

_____   _____
Account no.   Expiration Date

_____   _____
Signature   Date

_____   _____
Name   Title

_____
Mailing Address

_____   _____
City   State

_____   _____
Country   Zip/Postal Code

_____   _____
Phone   Fax

Faster Service: Fax your order to 918.832-9295

To validate this offer, please take a minute to answer the questions to the right. Thank you.

1. My Primary Business *(Please check ONE only)*
01 ❏ Imaging Services including Typesetting Services, Color Separators and Service Bureaus
03 ❏ Commercial Printer, including Printing Services, Instant/Quick Printers and Specialty Printers
05 ❏ Publishing (excluding newspapers)
07 ❏ Corporate/In-Plant, Non-commercial in-house services including: Printing services, Imaging services, Art/Graphic services and Reprographics services
09 ❏ Daily/Weekly Newspaper
13 ❏ Dealer/VAR/Systems Integrator
15 ❏ Military, Government Agency
17 ❏ Advertising Agency/Public Relations
19 ❏ Art/Graphic Service/Design Studio
23 ❏ Educational Institution
25 ❏ Manufacturers of products related to electronic publishing
27 ❏ Catalog Producers
31 ❏ Other (Please specify)_____

1. My Primary Job Function Is *(Please check ONE only)*
A ❏ Business Management (Pres., Owner, V.P., etc.)
B ❏ Production Management
C ❏ Dept. Supervision/Management
D ❏ Communications/Publishing Mgmt.
E ❏ MIS/DP
F ❏ Art Management
G ❏ Editorial Management
H ❏ Sales/Marketing Management
K ❏ Other Mgmt (Please specify)_____
X ❏ Other (Please specify)_____

Your source for all the latest information is Color Publishing.

If Mailing, Send To: Color Publishing • P.O. Box 3093 • Tulsa, OK 74101

A PENNWELL PUBLICATION

Work Smart

Look Good

Subscribe To Computer Artist!

✂ *Please cut and return for processing*

YES! I want to work smart and look good with Computer Artist. Enter a 1-year (6 issues) subscription at the special low rate of $24.95—almost 20% off the cover price! I understand that if I am disappointed in any way, I may write "cancel" on the invoice, but keep my FREE issue.

❑ Payment enclosed   Charge My: ❑ American Express ❑ Discover ❑ MasterCard ❑ EuroCard ❑ VISA ❑ Access

Account no.	Expiration Date
Signature	Date
Name	Title
Mailing Address	
City	State
Country	Zip/Postal Code
Phone	Fax

Faster Service: Fax your order to 918.832-9295
To validate this offer, please take a minute to answer the questions to the right. Thank you.

1. My Primary Business *(Please check ONE only)*
02 ❑ Commercial Art/Design (Ad Agency, Art studio, Graphic Design, Package Design)
06 ❑ Publishing (excluding newspaper) Book, Magazine, Catalog, Directory
10 ❑ Corporation/In-Plant (Non-Commercial Art/Design Services)
14 ❑ Newspaper Publishing (Daily, Weekly, Specialty)
18 ❑ Service Bureau (Color Separator, Imaging Service, Retouching House, Slide Services)
22 ❑ Creative/Production (Photography Studio, Video Production House, Multimedia Production, Presentation Graphics Services)
26 ❑ Direct Marketing Services
30 ❑ Dealer/VAR/Systems Integrator
34 ❑ Government
38 ❑ Educational Institution
46 ❑ Other (Please specify)_____

2. My Primary Job Function Is *(Please check ONE only)*
A ❑ Business Management (Pres., Owner, V.P., Director, etc.)
B ❑ Art Management/Creative Management
C ❑ Graphic Design
D ❑ Package/Industrial Art Design
E ❑ Presentation Graphics/Multimedia
F ❑ Photo Editing/Retouching
H ❑ Illustration/Technical Illustration
K ❑ Creative Consulting
N ❑ Educator
R ❑ Other (Please specify)_____

Your source for all the latest tips and techniques in digital imaging.

If Mailing, Send To: Computer Artist • P.O. Box 3188 • Tulsa, OK 74101

A PENNWELL PUBLICATION

DIGITAL DESIGN FOR THE 21ST CENTURY

You can count on Osborne/McGraw-Hill and its expert authors to bring you the inside scoop on digital design, production, and the best-selling graphics software.

Digital Images: A Practical Guide
by Adele Droblas Greenberg
and Seth Greenberg
$26.95 U.S.A.
ISBN 0-07-882113-4

Scanning the Professional Way
by Sybil Ihrig and Emil Ihrig
$21.95 U.S.A.
ISBN 0-07-882145-2

Preparing Digital Images for Print
by Sybil Ihrig and Emil Ihrig
$21.95 U.S.A.
ISBN 0-07-882146-0

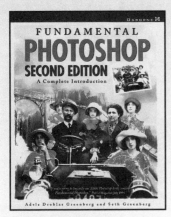

**Fundamental Photoshop:
A Complete Introduction,
Second Edition**
by Adele Droblas Greenberg
and Seth Greenberg
$29.95 U.S.A.
ISBN 0-07-882093-6

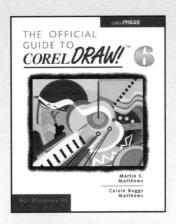

**The Official Guide to
CorelDRAW!™6 for Windows 95**
by Martin S. Matthews and Carole Boggs Matthews
$34.95 U.S.A.
ISBN 0-07-882168-1

**The Official Guide to Corel
PHOTO-PAINT 6**
by David Huss
$34.95 U.S.A.
ISBN 0-07-882207-6

ORDER BOOKS DIRECTLY FROM OSBORNE/McGRAW-HILL

For a complete catalog of Osborne's books, call 510-549-6600 or write to us at 2600 Tenth Street, Berkeley, CA 94710

☎ **Call Toll-Free,** *24 hours a day, 7 days a week, in the U.S.A. and Canada*
U.S.A.: 1-800-822-8158   **Canada: 1-800-565-5758**

✉ **Mail** *in the U.S.A. to:*
McGraw-Hill, Inc.
Customer Service Dept.
P.O. Box 547
Blacklick, OH 43004

Canada
McGraw-Hill Ryerson
Customer Service
300 Water Street
Whitby, Ontario L1N 9B6

Fax *in the U.S.A. to:*
1-614-759-3644

Canada
1-800-463-5885

orders@mcgraw-hill.ca

SHIP TO:

Name _____

Company _____

Address _____

City / State / Zip _____

Daytime Telephone *(We'll contact you if there's a question about your order.)*

ISBN #	BOOK TITLE	Quantity	Price	Total
0-07-88				
0-07-88				
0-07-88				
0-07-88				
0-07-88				
0-07088				
0-07-88				
0-07-88				
0-07-88				
0-07-88				
0-07-88				
0-07-88				
0-07-88				

Shipping & Handling Charge from Chart Below

Subtotal

Please Add Applicable State & Local Sales Tax

TOTAL

Shipping & Handling Charges

Order Amount	U.S.	Outside U.S.
$15.00 - $24.99	$4.00	$6.00
$25.00 - $49.99	$5.00	$7.00
$50.00 - $74.99	$6.00	$8.00
$75.00 - and up	$7.00	$9.00
$100 - and up	$8.00	$10.00

Occasionally we allow other selected companies to use our mailing list. If you would prefer that we not include you in these extra mailings, please check here: ☐

METHOD OF PAYMENT

☐ Check or money order enclosed (payable to Osborne/McGraw-Hill)

☐ AMERICAN EXPRESS   ☐ DISCOVER   ☐ MasterCard.   ☐ VISA

Account No. ☐☐☐☐☐☐☐☐☐☐☐☐☐☐☐☐

Expiration Date _____

Signature _____

In a hurry? Call 1-800-822-8158 anytime, day or night, or visit your local bookstore.

Thank you for your order   Code BC640SL